# BILL GRANGER
# HOLIDAY

**PHOTOGRAPHY BY PETRINA TINSLAY**

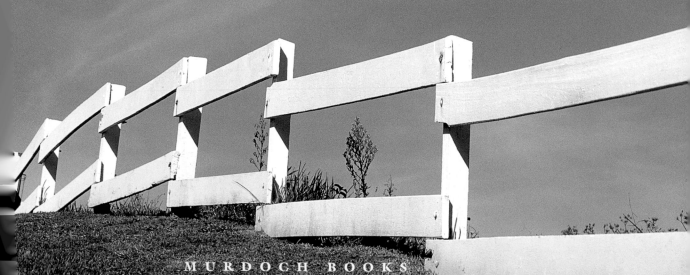

MURDOCH BOOKS

# CONTENTS

"For me, a holiday doesn't need to be about going away somewhere; it's very much a state of mind, a special feeling, a stolen moment, a happy accident. It's about kicking back and taking time out, or finding myself somewhere I didn't expect to be. My holidays are about laying down memories, and the way I do that almost always involves food. We all have those flashbacks to places, times, people that are brought about by the smell from a kitchen or the first mouthful of a dish. These are the recipes that have marked my life so far, that create instant snapshots in my mind. This food that I'm enjoying with my family will, hopefully, one day whisk my children back to their own magical moments."

Spring arrives and it's the **outdoors** call to spend less time in the kitchen and more in the fresh air. Flavours become clear and sharp and fresh. The farmers' markets start to buzz, heralding new arrivals that shout spring: thick fingers of asparagus, shiny, juicy cherries and sweet, sweet peas.

I'm one of those slightly annoying people who swears that food always tastes better outdoors. At the first hint of spring, when there's an ever-so-slight chill in the air, I'm sweeping the patio and shifting pots of herbs. We'll plant pansies and make cane tepees for hopeful tomato seedlings, the doors and windows flung open to the air and the sun. I set up elaborate spreads in the garden and invite friends over. And I absolutely love picnics. I'll pile the girls and their pink picnic sets into the car (or onto the pram that doubles as an all-purpose trolley) to have their sandwiches and home-made lemonade in the park.

The change of season and the first hint of spring always remind Natalie and me of a wonderful family holiday we had in the South of France. It was one of those remarkable trips where we felt as if we'd been spirited into a real-life advertisement for pasta sauce. Every day we would eat croissants collected from the local *boulangerie* and set off to explore markets packed with fresh spring produce at the top of steep cobblestoned streets that oozed history. We would sit on the terrace of our perfect eighteenth-century farmhouse, watching sheep graze under the pencil pines, and eat rotisserie chicken, pan-fried potatoes and salads of just-picked vegetables. (When I delve deeper into my subconscious, however, I can also discover memories of pushing a double pram up an impossible cobblestoned incline with a three-year-old wailing, 'Not the markets again, Daddy!' At that point the behemoth of a *supermarché* we had passed somewhere on the highway would flit alluringly across my mind. But those are the sorts of things that fade away, thankfully, with time. The photos of happy, cherry-juice-stained children help a lot, too.)

Although I see myself as an outdoors sort of person, I have had to come to terms with the fact that camping isn't really my thing. My one and only camping trip, when I was nineteen, ended in disaster, with bad weather, bad tempers, an almost-biblical plague of mosquitoes, and all our belongings being emergency Fed-Exed home. The poor watermelon I had taken with me (seriously!) was left behind, a sodden, broken mess. But one of the best things about the whole experience was the homecoming feast. To celebrate enduring a weekend under canvas we all went out for tuna pasta at Sydney's incomparable Mario's. Since then, thoughts of too-small tents and soggy groundsheets have been miraculously chased from my mind by visions of a sumptuous bowl of pasta with seared tuna, chilli, cherry tomatoes and olives.

# PICNIC

## ROAST BEEF SANDWICHES WITH OLIVE CAPER RELISH

**SERVES 8 WITH LEFTOVERS**

1.5 KG (3 LB 5 OZ) TOPSIDE ROAST
OLIVE OIL, TO DRIZZLE
SEA SALT
FRESHLY GROUND BLACK PEPPER

**TO SERVE**
SOURDOUGH BREAD, OR YOUR FAVOURITE SANDWICH BREAD
ROCKET (ARUGULA) LEAVES
OLIVE CAPER RELISH, BELOW

Preheat the oven to 220°C (425°F/Gas 7). Put the beef on a large baking tray, drizzle with olive oil and season with sea salt and pepper. Roast for 15 minutes, or until browned.

Reduce the oven temperature to 200°C (400°F/Gas 6) and roast the beef for a further 45 minutes (it will be medium-rare). Remove from the oven, cover loosely with foil and set aside to rest for 30 minutes. Thinly slice the beef and use to make sandwiches with the bread, rocket and olive caper relish.

## OLIVE CAPER RELISH

**SERVES 8**

120 G (4 OZ/1 CUP) PITTED GREEN OLIVES
1 TABLESPOON SMALL SALTED CAPERS, RINSED
2 TABLESPOONS CHOPPED FRESH FLAT-LEAF (ITALIAN) PARSLEY
2 TEASPOONS GRATED LEMON ZEST
3 TABLESPOONS EXTRA VIRGIN OLIVE OIL
FRESHLY GROUND BLACK PEPPER

Put the olives, capers, parsley and lemon zest in a food processor and finely chop. Add the olive oil and process until the relish has a coarse pesto-like consistency. Season with black pepper.

## GREEN RATATOUILLE

3 TABLESPOONS OLIVE OIL
3 LARGE ZUCCHINI (COURGETTES), DICED
1 WHITE ONION, DICED
2 GARLIC CLOVES, THINLY SLICED
4 CELERY STALKS, DICED
2 GREEN CAPSICUMS (PEPPERS), SEEDED AND DICED
2 TEASPOONS CHOPPED FRESH THYME LEAVES
SEA SALT
FRESHLY GROUND BLACK PEPPER

Preheat the oven to 180°C (350°F/Gas 4). Heat 1 tablespoon of the olive oil in a large frying pan over medium-high heat. Add the zucchini and cook, stirring occasionally, for 5–6 minutes or until light golden. Remove from the heat and tip into a large ovenproof dish.

Return the pan to medium heat and add the remaining oil. Add the onion, garlic, celery and capsicum and cook, stirring occasionally, for 6–7 minutes, or until the vegetables are softened. Add to the ovenproof dish and sprinkle with thyme leaves and salt and pepper. Cover with foil and bake for 25–30 minutes.

# POACHED SALMON AND RISONI SALAD

**SERVES 4–6**

1 TABLESPOON SALT
½ TEASPOON WHITE PEPPERCORNS
1 BAY LEAF
400 G (14 OZ) SALMON FILLETS, SKIN REMOVED
200 G (7 OZ) RISONI
85 G (3 OZ/½ CUP) PEAS (FROZEN ARE FINE)
GRATED ZEST AND JUICE OF 1 LEMON
55 G (2 OZ) BABY SPINACH LEAVES
2 TABLESPOONS CHOPPED FRESH FLAT-LEAF (ITALIAN) PARSLEY
2 TEASPOONS CHOPPED FRESH DILL
1 TABLESPOON EXTRA VIRGIN OLIVE OIL
A LARGE PINCH OF CASTER (SUPERFINE) SUGAR
FRESHLY GROUND BLACK PEPPER

Put the salt, peppercorns and bay leaf in a large deep frying pan with 750 ml (26 fl oz/3 cups) of water and bring to the boil. Simmer for 5 minutes, then remove from the heat. Add the salmon, cover and leave for 15 minutes. Lift the fish carefully out of the stock. When cool enough to handle, flake the fish into pieces, picking out any bones.

Cook the risoni in a large pan of boiling salted water until al dente, adding the peas and lemon zest for the last 2 minutes of cooking. Rinse under cold running water and drain well.

Put the risoni, peas, salmon, spinach, parsley and dill in a large bowl. Whisk together the lemon juice, olive oil and sugar to make a dressing. Add the dressing to the salad and toss gently. Season with sea salt and black pepper.

"Poaching the salmon in the stock off the heat is a great 'no-cook' method that results in very succulent fish."

"I bake my empanadas, but if there are traditionalists out there, feel free to shallow-fry these for a couple of minutes on each side."

# MUSHROOM AND RICOTTA EMPANADAS

**MAKES 12**

**PASTRY**
250 G (9 OZ/2 CUPS) PLAIN (ALL-PURPOSE) FLOUR
1 TEASPOON SALT
3 TABLESPOONS OLIVE OIL
1 EGG YOLK

**FILLING**
2 TABLESPOONS OLIVE OIL
1 ONION, FINELY CHOPPED
2 GARLIC CLOVES, CRUSHED
300 G (10½ OZ) SWISS BROWN MUSHROOMS, SLICED
3 LONG GREEN CHILLIES, SEEDED AND FINELY CHOPPED
SEA SALT
FRESHLY GROUND BLACK PEPPER
250 G (9 OZ/1 CUP) FRESH RICOTTA CHEESE
1 EGG YOLK, MIXED WITH 2 TABLESPOONS MILK

**TO SERVE**
FRESH CHILLI AND LIME RELISH, OVERLEAF
BLACK BEAN SALAD WITH LIME, CHILLI AND AVOCADO, OVERLEAF

To make the pastry, sift the flour and salt into a large bowl. Add the oil, egg yolk and 125 ml (4 fl oz/ ½ cup) of iced water. Mix with a fork until the dough comes together, adding a touch more water if necessary. Gather it up and transfer to a lightly floured surface. Knead until smooth and elastic. Divide the dough into 12 balls, cover with a clean damp cloth and leave to rest for 30 minutes.

Meanwhile, to make the filling, heat the olive oil in a large frying pan over medium-high heat. Add the onion and cook, stirring occasionally, for 6–7 minutes, or until the onion is soft. Add the garlic, mushrooms and chilli and cook, stirring occasionally, for 5 minutes. Season well and leave to cool.

Preheat your oven to 180°C (350°F/Gas 4). Roll out each ball of pastry on a lightly floured surface into a 10 cm (4 inch) circle. Spread some mushroom filling over one half of the pastry, then top with a couple of teaspoons of ricotta. Brush the edges with water and fold over to make a semi-circle. Press the pastry edges together with a fork. Repeat with the remaining pastry and filling. Place on a baking tray, brush the tops with the egg and milk mixture and bake for 25 minutes until crisp and golden. Serve hot or cold, with chilli and lime relish and black bean salad.

## FRESH CHILLI AND LIME RELISH

**SERVES 6**

1 WHITE ONION, FINELY CHOPPED
3 LONG GREEN CHILLIES, SEEDED AND FINELY CHOPPED
2 TABLESPOONS CHOPPED FRESH CORIANDER (CILANTRO)
2 TABLESPOONS LIME JUICE
½ TEASPOON SEA SALT
A PINCH OF CASTER (SUPERFINE) SUGAR

Stir together all the ingredients and leave for 10 minutes. This is lovely with grilled or barbecued meat and fish, but expecially good with empanadas.

## BLACK BEAN SALAD WITH LIME, CHILLI AND AVOCADO

**SERVES 6**

325 G (11 OZ/1½ CUPS) BLACK BEANS, SOAKED OVERNIGHT AND DRAINED
150 G (5½ OZ) GREEN BEANS, TOPPED
2 TABLESPOONS EXTRA VIRGIN OLIVE OIL
2 TABLESPOONS LIME JUICE
1 TEASPOON GROUND CUMIN
2 LONG GREEN CHILLIES, SEEDED AND FINELY CHOPPED
SEA SALT
FRESHLY GROUND BLACK PEPPER
6 SPRING ONIONS (SCALLIONS), FINELY SLICED
2 TABLESPOONS CHOPPED FRESH CORIANDER (CILANTRO)
1 AVOCADO, SLICED

Put the black beans in a large saucepan, cover with water and bring to the boil. Reduce the heat to low and simmer for 1 hour, or until tender but still with a little bite. Drain well.

Meanwhile, blanch the green beans in lightly salted boiling water until they are bright green and tender crisp. Rinse under cold running water and drain well. Cut into short lengths.

Put the warm black beans in a large bowl, add the olive oil, lime juice, cumin and chilli. Season with salt and pepper and leave to cool completely. Stir in the green beans, spring onion and coriander and top with slices of avocado.

## STICKY CHICKEN WINGS

SERVES 4

3 TABLESPOONS MIRIN
3 TABLESPOONS SOY SAUCE
2 TEASPOONS CASTER (SUPERFINE) SUGAR
1 TEASPOON GRATED FRESH GINGER
16 FREE-RANGE CHICKEN WINGS, TIPS REMOVED AND HALVED AT THE JOINTS
2 TEASPOONS SESAME SEEDS

TO SERVE
SOBA NOODLES DRESSED WITH A LITTLE SOY SAUCE AND MIRIN

Stir together the mirin, soy, sugar and ginger in a large shallow non-metallic dish. Add the chicken wings and coat thoroughly in the marinade. Cover and refrigerate for at least 2 hours.

Preheat your oven to 200°C (400°F/Gas 6). Lift the chicken wings out of the marinade (keeping the marinade) and place in a single layer in a large baking dish. Roast for 30 minutes, turning once.

Meanwhile, pour the marinade into a small pan. Bring to the boil and simmer until reduced by half. Pour the reduced marinade over the chicken wings, toss to coat and return to the oven for a further 10–15 minutes. Sprinkle the chicken with sesame seeds and bake for 5 minutes more until the chicken is sticky and golden and the sesame seeds are toasted. Delicious with soba noodles dressed with a little soy sauce and mirin.

"If you don't have time to marinate the wings beforehand, make and reduce the marinade, then just pour it over the wings halfway through roasting."

# ALMOND AND RASPBERRY SLICE

**MAKES 20 PIECES**

**210 G (7½ OZ) UNSALTED BUTTER, SOFTENED**
**165 G (5¾ OZ/¾ CUP) CASTER (SUPERFINE) SUGAR**
**2 TEASPOONS VANILLA EXTRACT**
**200 G (7 OZ) FLAKED ALMONDS**
**2 TABLESPOONS MILK**
**225 G (8 OZ/1¾ CUPS) PLAIN (ALL-PURPOSE) FLOUR**
**40 G (1½ OZ/⅓ CUP) CORNFLOUR (CORNSTARCH)**
**160 G (5½ OZ/½ CUP) RASPBERRY JAM**

Preheat the oven to 180°C (350°F/Gas 4). Lightly grease a 24 x 20 cm (9½ x 8 inch) baking tin and line with baking paper.

To make the almond topping, put 60 g (2½ oz) of the butter, 55 g (2 oz/¼ cup) of the sugar, 1 teaspoon vanilla extract, the almonds and milk in a saucepan. Cook over very low heat until the butter has melted, then leave to cool.

To make the base, beat the remaining butter, sugar and vanilla extract with electric beaters until pale and creamy. Sift the flour and cornflour together and add in two batches, beating on low speed until just mixed. Press the dough into the baking tin and bake for 12 minutes, or until light golden. Remove from the oven and leave to cool for 10 minutes.

Carefully spread the jam over the pastry base, then spread the cooled almond topping over the jam. Return to the oven and bake for a further 25 minutes, or until golden brown.

## PASSIONFRUIT MELTING MOMENTS

**MAKES ABOUT 15**

250 G (9 OZ) UNSALTED BUTTER, SOFTENED
60 G (2¼ OZ/½ CUP) ICING (CONFECTIONER'S) SUGAR
225 G (8 OZ/1¾ CUPS) PLAIN (ALL-PURPOSE) FLOUR
80 G (2¾ OZ/⅔ CUP) CORNFLOUR (CORNSTARCH)

**PASSIONFRUIT CREAM**
60 G (2¼ OZ) UNSALTED BUTTER, SOFTENED
125 G (4½ OZ/1 CUP) ICING (CONFECTIONER'S) SUGAR, SIFTED
1 TABLESPOON PASSIONFRUIT PULP

Preheat the oven to 170°C (325°F/Gas 3) and line 2 large baking trays with baking paper.

Cream the butter and sugar until pale and creamy. Sift together the flour and cornflour, add to the creamed mixture and beat well. (Alternatively, mix the sugar, flour and cornflour in a food processor, pulsing until combined. Add the softened butter and process until the mixture comes together.) With floured hands, take scant tablespoons of the mixture and roll into balls, put on the trays and flatten slightly with a fork dipped in flour. Bake for 15–18 minutes until light golden, then cool on a wire rack.

To make the passionfruit cream, beat the butter with electric beaters until completely smooth. Gradually add the icing sugar and continue beating until pale and creamy. Add the passionfruit pulp and beat well. Join the cooled biscuits together with the passionfruit cream.

"My auntie (a real old-fashioned country biscuit-maker) made the best melting moments. This is her recipe, although without the custard powder she liked to add. They might not be quite as yellow, but they're just as delicious."

## CRANBERRY AND WHITE CHOCOLATE COOKIES

MAKES 30

150 G (5½ OZ) UNSALTED BUTTER, SOFTENED
165 G (5¾ OZ/¾ CUP) FIRMLY PACKED BROWN SUGAR
1 EGG, LIGHTLY BEATEN
2 TEASPOONS VANILLA EXTRACT
125 G (4½ OZ/1 CUP) PLAIN (ALL-PURPOSE) FLOUR
1 TEASPOON BAKING POWDER
A PINCH OF SALT
200 G (7 OZ/2 CUPS) ROLLED OATS
140 G (5 OZ/1 CUP) WHITE CHOCOLATE CHUNKS
85 G (3 OZ/⅔ CUP) DRIED CRANBERRIES

Preheat the oven to 180°C (350°F/Gas 4) and line 3 baking trays with baking paper.

Cream the butter and sugar together until pale and creamy. Add the egg and vanilla and beat until smooth. Sift the flour, baking powder and salt together. Add the oats, chocolate and cranberries and stir together. Add to the creamed mixture and stir together well.

Roll small tablespoons of the mixture into balls and place on the baking trays. Flatten the balls with a fork dipped in flour. Bake for 12–15 minutes until pale golden. Leave to cool on the trays for 5 minutes before transferring to a wire rack to cool completely.


## PINK LEMONADE

SERVES 6

115 G (4 OZ/½ CUP) CASTER (SUPERFINE) SUGAR
250 ML (9 FL OZ/1 CUP) CRANBERRY JUICE
250 ML (9 FL OZ/1 CUP) FRESH LEMON JUICE
750 ML (26 FL OZ/3 CUPS) SODA WATER

Put the sugar and 125 ml (4 fl oz/½ cup) of water in a saucepan and stir over low heat until the sugar has dissolved. Remove from the heat and leave to cool. Mix the sugar syrup with the cranberry juice, lemon juice and soda water and stir together well.

# TERRACE DINING

## CRISP ZUCCHINI FLOWERS

**SERVES 4 AS A STARTER**

125 G (4½ OZ/1 CUP) PLAIN (ALL-PURPOSE) FLOUR
2 TEASPOONS CURRY POWDER
1 TEASPOON BAKING POWDER
SEA SALT
FRESHLY GROUND BLACK PEPPER
ABOUT 125 ML (4 FL OZ/½ CUP) SPARKLING MINERAL WATER
OLIVE OIL, TO SHALLOW-FRY
12 ZUCCHINI (COURGETTE) FLOWERS, STAMENS REMOVED

Sift the flour, curry powder and baking powder into a large mixing bowl and season with salt and pepper. Make a well in the centre and then whisk in enough sparkling mineral water to make a very runny, smooth batter.

Heat enough olive oil to come 5 cm (2 inches) up the side of a shallow saucepan over high heat (I like to use my flat-bottomed wok). Dip the zucchini flowers into the batter, in batches, allowing the excess to drip off.

Carefully lower the zucchini flowers into the hot oil and fry, a few at a time, until golden brown. Remove with a slotted spoon and drain on kitchen paper.

"If your greengrocer doesn't stock zucchini flowers, or if they aren't in season, you can also make these with batons of zucchini."

## CHICKEN WITH HERBES DE PROVENCE

**SERVES 4**

**1 X 1.6 KG (3 LB 8 OZ) FREE-RANGE CHICKEN**
**OLIVE OIL, TO DRIZZLE**
**SEA SALT**
**FRESHLY GROUND BLACK PEPPER**
**2 TEASPOONS HERBES DE PROVENCE**

Wash the chicken inside and out and pat dry with kitchen paper. To spatchcock the chicken, place the bird, breast side down, on a board. Using poultry shears or a sharp knife, cut along both sides of the backbone, cutting through the skin and bone. Remove the backbone. Turn the bird over and press firmly on the breastbone to break the bone and flatten the breast. Tuck the wing tips under the breast.

Preheat your oven to 220°C (425°F/Gas 7) or preheat a covered barbecue.

Cut five deep slashes into the flesh on the legs and thighs of the chicken and three slashes along each side of the breast. Drizzle with olive oil, season with salt and pepper and sprinkle with the herbs.

Put the chicken in a large roasting tin, breast side up, and roast for 45 minutes. Leave to rest for 5 minutes before carving. To barbecue, place the chicken, breast side up, on the barbecue, cover with the lid and cook for 45–50 minutes.

## POTATOES WITH ONION AND PANCETTA

SERVES 4–6

3 TABLESPOONS OLIVE OIL
50 G (1¾ OZ) BUTTER
2 WHITE ONIONS, CUT INTO WEDGES
1 KG (2 LB 4 OZ) YELLOW WAXY POTATOES (SUCH AS KIPFLER), PEELED AND THINLY SLICED
150 G (5½ OZ) PIECE OF PANCETTA, CUT INTO THIN STRIPS
SEA SALT
FRESHLY GROUND BLACK PEPPER
3 TABLESPOONS FINELY CHOPPED FRESH FLAT-LEAF (ITALIAN) PARSLEY

Heat the oil and butter in a large deep non-stick frying pan or flat-bottomed wok over medium heat. Add the onion, potato and pancetta and stir together. Cover with the lid and cook, stirring occasionally, for 20 minutes, or until just soft.

Increase the heat to medium-high, remove the lid and cook, stirring occasionally, for a further 15–20 minutes, or until the potatoes are golden. Season well with sea salt and freshly ground black pepper. Sprinkle with the parsley and toss well.

## TOMATO, CAPER, BASIL AND CROUTON SALAD

SERVES 6

3 TABLESPOONS EXTRA VIRGIN OLIVE OIL
1 GARLIC CLOVE, CRUSHED
4 THICK SLICES DAY-OLD SOURDOUGH BREAD, DICED
4 RIPE TOMATOES, DICED
2 TEASPOONS SMALL SALTED CAPERS, RINSED
A PINCH OF CASTER (SUPERFINE) SUGAR
A HANDFUL OF FRESH BASIL LEAVES
1 LEMON, PEEL AND PITH REMOVED, DIVIDED INTO SEGMENTS
SEA SALT
FRESHLY GROUND BLACK PEPPER

Preheat the oven to 170°C (325°F/Gas 3). Mix 2 tablespoons of the olive oil with the garlic. Toss the bread in the garlic oil, arrange on a baking tray and bake until golden.

Toss together the tomatoes and capers in a large serving bowl, add the remaining olive oil and sugar and toss again. Add the croutons, basil leaves and lemon segments, season with salt and pepper and toss gently before serving.

## CHERRY TART

SERVES 8–10

**PASTRY**
125 G (4½ OZ) UNSALTED BUTTER, MELTED AND COOLED
90 G (3½ OZ) CASTER (SUPERFINE) SUGAR
175 G (6 OZ) PLAIN (ALL-PURPOSE) FLOUR
A PINCH OF SALT
2 TABLESPOONS ALMOND MEAL (GROUND ALMONDS)

**FILLING**
170 ML (5½ FL OZ/⅔ CUP) CREAM
2 EGGS, LIGHTLY BEATEN
2 TEASPOONS VANILLA EXTRACT
3 TABLESPOONS CASTER (SUPERFINE) SUGAR
2 TABLESPOONS PLAIN (ALL-PURPOSE) FLOUR
550 G (1 LB 4 OZ) CHERRIES, HALVED AND PITTED (FRESH ARE BEST)

Preheat the oven to 180°C (350°F/Gas 4) and grease a 24 cm (9½ inch) round loose-bottomed tart tin. To make the pastry, stir together the butter and sugar in a large mixing bowl. Add the flour and salt and stir to make a soft dough. Transfer the dough to the tin and press evenly into the base and side of the tin with your fingertips. Put the tin on a baking tray and bake for 12–15 minutes, or until the pastry is slightly puffy. Remove from the oven and sprinkle the almond meal over the base.

Meanwhile, to make the filling, whisk together the cream, eggs, vanilla and sugar. Add the flour and whisk until well mixed. Arrange the cherries, slightly overlapping, over the pastry base and pour the cream filling evenly over the cherries.

Return the tart to the oven for a further 40–50 minutes until the filling is firm. Leave to cool and serve with cream or ice cream.

"This pastry is inspired by Patricia Wells. It's an absolute dream to make because it uses melted butter (so no need to drag out the food processor)."

"Fresh cherries are always going to be best, but you could get away with frozen at a pinch. The almond meal absorbs any liquid from the cherries and keeps the pastry crisp."

# AND WITH THE LEFTOVER ROAST CHICKEN...

## CHORIZO AND SHREDDED CHICKEN TORTILLAS

SERVES 4

2 TEASPOONS OLIVE OIL
2 CHORIZO SAUSAGES, REMOVED FROM CASINGS, FILLING CRUMBLED
1 ONION, FINELY CHOPPED
1/4 SAVOY CABBAGE, FINELY SHREDDED
2 GARLIC CLOVES, CRUSHED
3 LONG RED CHILLIES, SEEDED AND CHOPPED
5 TOMATOES, CHOPPED
ABOUT 2 CUPS SHREDDED COOKED CHICKEN
125 ML (4 FL OZ/1/2 CUP) CHICKEN STOCK
SEA SALT
FRESHLY GROUND BLACK PEPPER

TO SERVE
FLOUR TORTILLAS
2 AVOCADOES, DICED
2 TABLESPOONS CHOPPED FRESH CORIANDER (CILANTRO)
2 TABLESPOONS LIME JUICE
GRILLED TOMATO AND CHILLI SALSA, BELOW

Heat the olive oil in a large pan over medium-high heat and cook the chorizo, stirring, for
4–5 minutes until golden. Add the onion and cook, stirring occasionally, for 5 minutes or until soft.
Add the cabbage, garlic and chilli and cook for 5 minutes or until the cabbage is soft. Add the
tomatoes and simmer for 10–15 minutes until they are falling apart. Add the chicken and stock and
simmer for 10 minutes or until most of the liquid has disappeared. Season with salt and pepper. Fill
the tortillas with the chicken filling. Mix together the avocado, coriander and lime juice and spoon
over the tortillas. Serve with grilled tomato and chilli salsa.

## GRILLED TOMATO AND CHILLI SALSA

3 LARGE RIPE TOMATOES
2 LARGE GREEN CHILLIES
1 GARLIC CLOVE, CRUSHED
2 TABLESPOONS EXTRA VIRGIN OLIVE OIL
1/2 TEASPOON CASTER (SUPERFINE) SUGAR

Preheat a grill (broiler) to high. Put the whole tomatoes and chillies on a baking tray and grill,
turning once, until they are lightly charred all over. Set aside to cool slightly. Peel the tomatoes, scoop
out the seeds and roughly chop the flesh. Peel and finely chop the chillies. Stir together the tomato,
chilli, garlic and olive oil in a serving bowl. Season with sugar, salt and pepper to taste.

# SPRING PASTA

## SPAGHETTI WITH ASPARAGUS, MINT AND CHILLI

**SERVES 4**

400 G (14 OZ) SPAGHETTI
80 ML (2¾ FL OZ/⅓ CUP) EXTRA VIRGIN OLIVE OIL
3 GARLIC CLOVES, THINLY SLICED
1 LONG RED CHILLI, SEEDED AND FINELY SLICED
2 BUNCHES OF ASPARAGUS (ABOUT 400 G/14 OZ), THINLY SLICED
A HANDFUL OF FRESH MINT LEAVES
SEA SALT
FRESHLY GROUND BLACK PEPPER

**TO SERVE**
GRATED PARMESAN

Cook the spaghetti in a large pan of lightly salted boiling water according to the packet instructions or until al dente. Reserve half a cupful of the cooking liquid before draining the pasta.

Meanwhile, heat the olive oil in a large frying pan over medium heat. Add the garlic and chilli and cook, stirring, for 30 seconds. Add the asparagus and continue to cook, stirring, for 1–2 minutes or until it is bright green and tender crisp. Add the pasta cooking liquid and simmer for 30 seconds.

Add the hot pasta and mint leaves to the asparagus and toss together. Season and serve immediately with grated parmesan.

"I have a pretty easy rule for pasta: dried pasta for light olive oil-based sauces and fresh pasta for soaking up the heavier wintery sauces."

# PENNE WITH TUNA, CHERRY TOMATOES AND OLIVES

**SERVES 4**

400 G (14 OZ) PENNE
125 ML (4 FL OZ/½ CUP) OLIVE OIL
500 G (1 LB 2 OZ) TUNA STEAK, DICED
2 GARLIC CLOVES, VERY THINLY SLICED
2 LONG RED CHILLIES, SEEDED AND FINELY CHOPPED
4 ANCHOVIES, CHOPPED
500 G (1 LB 2 OZ) CHERRY TOMATOES
A LARGE HANDFUL OF SMALL BLACK (NICOISE) OLIVES
A HANDFUL OF BASIL LEAVES, TORN
SEA SALT
FRESHLY GROUND BLACK PEPPER

Cook the pasta in a large pan of lightly salted boiling water according to the packet instructions or until al dente. Drain well.

Meanwhile, heat 1 tablespoon of the oil in a large frying pan over high heat. Add the tuna and cook, stirring occasionally, for 2–3 minutes until seared. Remove from the pan and set aside.

Return the pan to high heat, add the rest of the oil, the garlic, chilli and anchovies. Cook, stirring, for 1 minute. Add the tomatoes and olives and cook, stirring occasionally, for a further 5 minutes, or until the tomatoes are slightly softened.

Add the hot pasta and tuna to the pan and gently toss. Add the basil leaves and season with salt and pepper. Serve immediately.

## TAGLIATELLE WITH FRESH PEAS AND LEMON

SERVES 4

1½ TABLESPOONS OLIVE OIL
1½ TABLESPOONS BUTTER
2 GARLIC CLOVES, CRUSHED
185 ML (6 FL OZ/¾ CUP) WHITE WINE
1 TEASPOON FINELY GRATED LEMON ZEST
125 ML (4 FL OZ/½ CUP) CREAM
SEA SALT
FRESHLY GROUND BLACK PEPPER
400 G (14 OZ) TAGLIATELLE
300 G (10½ OZ/2 CUPS) FRESH SHELLED PEAS

**TO SERVE**
GRATED PARMESAN

Heat the oil and butter in a large frying pan over medium heat. Add the garlic and cook, stirring, for 1 minute. Add the white wine and simmer until reduced by half. Add the lemon zest and cream and simmer for a further 3–4 minutes until slightly reduced. Season with salt and pepper.

Meanwhile, cook the pasta in a large pan of lightly salted boiling water according to the packet instructions or until al dente, adding the peas for the last 3 minutes of the cooking time. Drain well and toss the hot pasta with the sauce. Serve immediately with grated parmesan.

"Fresh peas are so wonderfully evocative of spring, and another ingredient we seem to bypass in our modern lives. In an ideal world, we'd all spend half an hour a week on the back doorstep, shelling peas."

Didn't we all love those long days of the school summer holidays? When everything was bleached by the sun barefoot and we had to run through sprinklers to cool down. It's a real Aussie tradition to decamp to a beach shack where, because the stove is a hundred years old, every meal has to be cooked on the barbie.

My dad had a bright orange barbecue that consistently worked miracles — every single item that came out of it was charred black on the outside but remained basically raw on the inside. I like to think it was because of the poor barbecue technology of those days, but I'm not entirely convinced. Steak and sausages were always served with 'condiments' — a selection of tomato sauce, Worcestershire sauce and hot English mustard. And 'salad' was iceberg lettuce, tinned beetroot and green tomatoes, cold from the fridge. And always, always coleslaw. Despite this, grilled food with salad is still my favourite way to eat and, as Natalie and my best friend, Robert, will attest, I have a real soft spot for coleslaw, which I have resurrected in countless guises. Every time I suggest it, Nat smiles and tries very hard not to roll her eyes.

Many many countries have a tradition of grilled meats, yet Australians try to claim the barbecue as our own — I think we're being a bit cheeky, but perhaps that's part of our national character.

Because Dad was self-employed as a butcher and farmer, we couldn't head off to the beach for the summer like a lot of my school friends. But Mum and Dad did have the first pool in our street, so every day we'd have all the neighbourhood kids round for the full eight hours, dive-bombing and splashing. Several times a day we'd trek to the local corner store in search of lurid coloured ice blocks. I can vividly remember that feeling of darting home barefoot, trying to avoid burns from the scorching footpath, with my ice block melting fast and dripping down my arm. Dinner in those seventies summer days was often a paper-wrapped parcel of fish and chips with salt and vinegar, eaten on the side of the pool. Between mouthfuls I'd have to lie down on my tummy on the hot 'pebble-crete' to warm up because I'd spent too long in the cold water.

This past summer has been spent almost entirely playing with my new ice cream maker. This Christmas present from my daughters (which, I tease them, is a little like buying your wife a vacuum cleaner for Mother's Day), they insist is the 'best present they've ever given'. I like my ice creams fresh and simple; nothing should be overcomplicated in the summer and I never feel much like making custard bases in hot weather. (Incidentally, I do recommend getting an ice cream maker for another reason, not so obvious: when you are entertaining a group that includes children you might find, as we have done, up to eight of them crowded silently around the machine for a good hour, watching it churn and churn and churn...)

# BEACH BARBECUES

## PAPRIKA- AND OREGANO-MARINATED FISH WITH CHERRY TOMATO SALSA

SERVES 4

4 X 150 G (5 OZ) FILLETS OF FIRM FISH, SUCH AS TUNA, BLUE-EYE OR KINGFISH
JUICE OF 1 LEMON
3 TABLESPOONS OLIVE OIL, PLUS EXTRA FOR COOKING
2 GARLIC CLOVES, CRUSHED
2 TABLESPOONS CHOPPED FRESH OREGANO
1 TEASPOON PAPRIKA
1 TEASPOON SMOKED SPANISH PAPRIKA

**TO SERVE**
CHERRY TOMATO SALSA, BELOW
LEMON WEDGES

Place the fish in a shallow non-metallic container. Mix together the lemon juice, olive oil, garlic, oregano and paprika. Pour the marinade over the fish to coat, cover the dish with plastic wrap and refrigerate for 30 minutes.

Preheat your barbecue or chargrill pan to high and spray or brush lightly with olive oil. Add the fish and barbecue for 2 minutes on each side (for medium) or longer if you prefer. Serve with a spoonful of cherry tomato salsa and a chargrilled lemon wedge.

## CHERRY TOMATO SALSA

250 G (9 OZ) CHERRY TOMATOES, QUARTERED
4 SPRING ONIONS (SCALLIONS), THINLY SLICED
1 TABLESPOON CHOPPED FRESH OREGANO
1 LONG RED CHILLI, SEEDED AND FINELY CHOPPED
1 TABLESPOON SHERRY VINEGAR OR RED WINE VINEGAR
SEA SALT
FRESHLY GROUND BLACK PEPPER

Toss together all the ingredients and season with sea salt and freshly ground black pepper.

# LAMB SKEWERS WITH MINT AND GARLIC YOGHURT

**SERVES 4**

250 ML (9 FL OZ/1 CUP) THICK GREEK YOGHURT
2 GARLIC CLOVES, CRUSHED
1 TEASPOON GROUND CUMIN
2 TEASPOONS GROUND CORIANDER
JUICE OF 1 LEMON
700 G (1 LB 5 OZ) LAMB LEG, DICED
OLIVE OIL

**MINT AND GARLIC YOGHURT**
185 ML (6 FL OZ/¾ CUP) THICK GREEK YOGHURT
1 TABLESPOON CHOPPED FRESH CORIANDER (CILANTRO)
1 TABLESPOON CHOPPED FRESH MINT
1 TEASPOON GRATED LEMON ZEST
1 GARLIC CLOVE, CRUSHED

Mix together the yoghurt, garlic, cumin, coriander and lemon juice in a large non-metallic dish. Add the diced lamb and stir to coat well, then cover and refrigerate for at least 2 hours. Meanwhile, soak 12 wooden skewers in water for a while (this will prevent them scorching).

Preheat your barbecue or chargrill pan to high and brush lightly with oil. Thread the lamb cubes onto the skewers and cook for 2–3 minutes each side until lightly charred and cooked to your taste.

To make the mint and garlic yoghurt, stir together all the ingredients and season to taste. Serve the lamb skewers drizzled with a little mint and garlic yoghurt.

## PORK CUTLETS IN HOISIN AND GINGER MARINADE

SERVES 4

80 ML (2¾ FL OZ/⅓ CUP) HOISIN SAUCE
2 TABLESPOONS SOY SAUCE
2 TABLESPOONS OLIVE OIL, PLUS EXTRA TO BRUSH
1 TABLESPOON HONEY
2 TEASPOONS GRATED FRESH GINGER
2 GARLIC CLOVES, CRUSHED
4 PORK LOIN CUTLETS

Stir together the hoisin sauce, soy sauce, olive oil, honey, ginger and garlic in a shallow
non-metallic dish. Add the pork and stir well. Cover and marinate in the fridge for at least 2 hours.

Preheat your barbecue or chargrill pan to high heat and brush with olive oil. Cook the pork cutlets
for 3–4 minutes on each side, or until cooked to your liking.

## CHICKEN IN FRESH HERB MARINADE

SERVES 4–6

A LARGE HANDFUL OF FRESH CORIANDER (CILANTRO)
A LARGE HANDFUL OF FRESH FLAT-LEAF (ITALIAN) PARSLEY
A LARGE HANDFUL OF FRESH MINT
2 LONG RED CHILLIES, SEEDED AND CHOPPED
2 GARLIC CLOVES, CRUSHED
80 ML (2¾ FL OZ/⅓ CUP) OLIVE OIL
SEA SALT
FRESHLY GROUND BLACK PEPPER
1 X 1.6 KG (3 LB 8 OZ) FREE-RANGE CHICKEN, CUT INTO 8 PIECES

Put the coriander, parsley, mint, chilli, garlic and olive oil in a food processor and process
until smooth. Season to taste. Cut deep slashes in the chicken flesh, put in a large dish and pour the
marinade over the top. Toss together well and rub the marinade into the slashes.

Preheat your barbecue or chargrill pan to high heat and cook the chicken for about 8 minutes on
each side, or until it is lightly charred and cooked through.

# WHOLE GRILLED FISH WITH CURRY PASTE

**SERVES 4**

**1.5 KG (3 LB 5 OZ) WHOLE SNAPPER, CLEANED, GUTTED AND SCALED**
**1 LIME, SLICED, PLUS 1 TABLESPOON LIME JUICE**
**2 TABLESPOONS RED CURRY PASTE**
**2 TABLESPOONS GRAPESEED OIL (OR OTHER LIGHT-FLAVOURED OIL)**
**SEA SALT**
**FRESHLY GROUND BLACK PEPPER**

**TO SERVE**
**STEAMED RICE**
**LIME WEDGES**

Using a sharp knife, make four or five diagonal cuts in each side of the fish. Push the lime slices into the cavity of the fish. Mix together the red curry paste and lime juice and spread over both sides of the fish. Leave to marinate for at least 30 minutes.

Arrange two large pieces of foil slightly overlapping on your work surface and drizzle with half the oil. Put the fish in the middle of the foil, season with salt and pepper and drizzle with the remaining oil. Wrap the fish up well in the foil, then wrap another layer of foil around it.

Preheat your barbecue or chargrill to medium-high. Cook the fish for 7–8 minutes on each side, or until the flesh shows white and firm through the cuts you made. Serve with steamed rice.

"I haven't yet mastered grilling a whole fish on the barbie without foil: mine always seem to fall apart. So, if you're clever enough to do away with the foil, go for it. I love that delicious charred flavour."

"Even when I'm barbecuing, I like to keep the flavours of the meal simple and consistent. So, no Greek salads with Thai-style fish!"

## CHICKEN BURGERS WITH LEMONGRASS AND LIME

**SERVES 6**

600 G (1 LB 5 OZ) MINCED (GROUND) CHICKEN
1 ONION, FINELY GRATED
85 G (3 OZ/1 CUP) FRESH WHITE BREADCRUMBS
1 GARLIC CLOVE, CRUSHED
1 LEMONGRASS STALK, WHITE PART ONLY, FINELY CHOPPED
2 TABLESPOONS CHOPPED FRESH CORIANDER (CILANTRO)
2 TEASPOONS FINELY GRATED LIME ZEST
1 TABLESPOON FISH SAUCE
2 TEASPOONS CASTER (SUPERFINE) SUGAR

**TO SERVE**
**SOFT ROLLS**
**LETTUCE LEAVES**
**FRESH MINT AND CORIANDER (CILANTRO) LEAVES**
**CHILLI SAUCE**
**SPICY SLAW, OPPOSITE**

Put the chicken mince, onion, breadcrumbs, garlic, lemongrass, coriander, lime zest, fish sauce and sugar in a large bowl and mix together well with your hands. Shape into 6 patties, then cover and refrigerate for 30 minutes.

Preheat a barbecue or chargrill pan and brush with a little light-flavoured oil such as grapeseed or canola. Cook the patties for 4 minutes each side or until cooked through. Serve on soft rolls with lettuce, mint and coriander leaves and chilli sauce. Great with spicy slaw.

"If your butcher doesn't have any chicken mince, you can buy boneless thighs and mince them yourself in a food processor."

## SPICY SLAW

**SERVES 10**

2 TABLESPOONS CASTER (SUPERFINE) SUGAR
2 TABLESPOONS RICE VINEGAR OR WHITE VINEGAR
2 LARGE CARROTS, PEELED AND CUT INTO THIN MATCHSTICKS
2 LARGE HANDFULS SHREDDED WHITE CABBAGE
2 LARGE HANDFULS SHREDDED RED CABBAGE
4 CELERY STALKS, TRIMMED, CUT INTO THIN MATCHSTICKS
1 LARGE RED ONION, THINLY SLICED
1 LARGE HANDFUL FRESH VIETNAMESE MINT LEAVES (OR ORDINARY MINT LEAVES)
1 LARGE HANDFUL FRESH CORIANDER (CILANTRO) LEAVES

**SWEET CHILLI DRESSING**
1 TABLESPOON RICE VINEGAR OR WHITE VINEGAR
1 TABLESPOON CASTER (SUPERFINE) SUGAR
1½ TABLESPOONS LIME JUICE
2 TABLESPOONS FISH SAUCE
2 LONG RED CHILLIES, SEEDED AND FINELY CHOPPED
½ TEASPOON SALT

Mix together the sugar and rice vinegar, add the carrot and leave to marinate for 20 minutes.

Put the white and red cabbage in a large mixing bowl. Drain the carrot and add to the cabbage with the celery, onion, mint and coriander.

Mix together all the dressing ingredients, stirring until the sugar has dissolved. Add the dressing to the salad and toss together. Serve immediately.

"Anyone who knows me well knows I'm a great fan of 'real' burgers. These spicy chicken patties are definitely my this-summer's-favourite."

## SPICY RICE NOODLE SALAD WITH CUCUMBER AND CASHEWS

SERVES 4–6

200 G (7 OZ) DRIED RICE STICK NOODLES
1 TEASPOON GRAPESEED OIL (OR OTHER LIGHT-FLAVOURED OIL)
150 G (5½ OZ) SNOW PEAS (MANGETOUT), TRIMMED AND THINLY SLICED LENGTHWAYS
1 LEBANESE CUCUMBER, HALVED AND THINLY SLICED
A HANDFUL OF FRESH THAI BASIL (OR ORDINARY BASIL) LEAVES
A HANDFUL OF FRESH MINT LEAVES
4 TABLESPOONS CHOPPED CASHEW NUTS, LIGHTLY TOASTED

**DRESSING**
1 SMALL RED CHILLI, CHOPPED
1 RED ASIAN SHALLOT, ROUGHLY CHOPPED
1 GARLIC CLOVE, CHOPPED
1 TEASPOON FINELY GRATED FRESH GINGER
2 TABLESPOONS LIME JUICE
1½ TABLESPOONS FISH SAUCE
2 TEASPOONS BROWN SUGAR

To make the dressing, pound the chilli, shallot, garlic and ginger into a paste with a mortar and pestle. Add the lime juice, fish sauce and sugar and stir until the sugar has dissolved.

Put the rice noodles in a large heatproof bowl. Pour in enough boiling water to cover them and leave to soak for 10 minutes, or until softened. Rinse under cold water, drain well and toss with the oil. Blanch the snow peas in boiling water for 30 seconds or until bright green and tender crisp. Rinse under cold water and drain well. Add the snow peas, cucumber and herbs to the rice noodles. Toss with the dressing, sprinkle with cashews and serve immediately.

## TOMATO AND CORIANDER SALAD WITH SOY AND VINEGAR

SERVES 4–6

1 TABLESPOON LIGHT SOY SAUCE
1 TABLESPOON CHINESE BLACK VINEGAR (OR BALSAMIC VINEGAR)
2 TEASPOONS GRAPESEED OIL (OR OTHER LIGHT-FLAVOURED OIL)
1 TEASPOON CASTER (SUPERFINE) SUGAR
6 RIPE TOMATOES, CHOPPED
2 LEBANESE CUCUMBERS, CHOPPED
1 SMALL RED ONION, THINLY SLICED INTO RINGS
A HANDFUL OF FRESH CORIANDER (CILANTRO) LEAVES

Mix together the soy sauce, vinegar, oil and sugar, stirring until the sugar has dissolved. Toss together the tomato, cucumber and onion. Add the dressing and coriander and toss again before serving.

## FRESH TOMATO SALAD WITH GREEN CHILLI

SERVES 4–6

4 RIPE TOMATOES, THINLY SLICED
1 LONG GREEN CHILLI, SEEDED AND FINELY CHOPPED
3 SPRING ONIONS (SCALLIONS), WHITE PART ONLY, FINELY SLICED
2 TABLESPOONS EXTRA VIRGIN OLIVE OIL
1 TABLESPOON RED WINE VINEGAR
A PINCH OF CASTER (SUPERFINE) SUGAR
SEA SALT
FRESHLY GROUND BLACK PEPPER

Arrange the tomato slices, slightly overlapping, on a serving platter. Mix together the chilli, spring onions, olive oil, vinegar and sugar and stir until the sugar has dissolved. Spoon over the tomatoes and season with sea salt and freshly ground black pepper.

## CAULIFLOWER SALAD WITH OLIVES AND CAPERS

SERVES 4

3 TABLESPOONS EXTRA VIRGIN OLIVE OIL
1½ TABLESPOONS RED WINE VINEGAR
A SMALL HANDFUL OF GREEN OLIVES, PITTED AND FINELY DICED
1 TABLESPOON TINY SALTED CAPERS, RINSED AND FINELY CHOPPED
3 CORNICHONS (GHERKINS), FINELY DICED
3 SPRING ONIONS (SCALLIONS), WHITE PART ONLY, THINLY SLICED
2 TABLESPOONS CHOPPED FRESH FLAT-LEAF (ITALIAN) PARSLEY
½ TEASPOON DRIED CHILLI FLAKES
SEA SALT
FRESHLY GROUND BLACK PEPPER
750 G (1 LB 10 OZ) CAULIFLOWER, CUT INTO SMALL FLORETS

To make the dressing, whisk the olive oil and red wine vinegar together in a small bowl. Add the olives, capers, cornichons, spring onions, parsley and chilli. Season with salt and pepper.

Blanch the cauliflower in a large saucepan of lightly salted water for 3–4 minutes until tender crisp. Drain well. While the cauliflower is still warm, put it in a large serving bowl, add the dressing and toss gently. Serve warm or cold.

# EGGPLANT SALAD WITH CHILLI AND MINT

SERVES 4–6

3 LARGE EGGPLANTS (AUBERGINES)
2 TABLESPOONS EXTRA VIRGIN OLIVE OIL
2 TABLESPOONS RED WINE VINEGAR
1 LONG RED CHILLI, SEEDED, FINELY CHOPPED
3 TABLESPOONS SHREDDED FRESH MINT LEAVES
3 TABLESPOONS SHREDDED FRESH FLAT-LEAF (ITALIAN) PARSLEY
SEA SALT
FRESHLY GROUND BLACK PEPPER

Cut each eggplant into thick slices. Preheat a barbecue or chargrill pan to high and cook the eggplant for 2–3 minutes on each side or until lightly charred and cooked through. Transfer to a heatproof bowl, cover with plastic wrap and set aside for 15 minutes.

Meanwhile, whisk together the olive oil and red wine vinegar in a small bowl. Add the chilli, mint, and parsley, season with salt and pepper and stir together.

Tear the eggplant into rough strips with your fingers and place in a serving bowl. Add the dressing and gently toss together.

# CARROT SALAD WITH OLIVES, HONEY AND CUMIN

SERVES 4

3 CARROTS, PEELED AND COARSELY GRATED OR VERY FINELY SLICED
1 SMALL RED CHILLI, SEEDED AND FINELY CHOPPED
2 TABLESPOONS CHOPPED FRESH CORIANDER (CILANTRO)
A HANDFUL OF SMALL BLACK OLIVES, PITTED
SEA SALT
FRESHLY GROUND BLACK PEPPER
2 TABLESPOONS EXTRA VIRGIN OLIVE OIL
1 TABLESPOON LEMON JUICE
1 TEASPOON RUNNY HONEY
1 TEASPOON GROUND CUMIN

Put the carrot, chilli, coriander and olives in a large bowl, season with salt and pepper and toss together well. Whisk together the olive oil, lemon juice, honey and cumin. Add the dressing to the salad and toss well.

# ICE CREAMS

## YOGHURT AND RASPBERRY ICE CREAM

**SERVES 4–6**

100 G (3½ OZ) CASTER (SUPERFINE) SUGAR
500 G (1 LB 2 OZ) THICK GREEK YOGHURT
115 G (4 OZ) PUNNET OF FRESH RASPBERRIES

Whisk the sugar and yoghurt together until well combined. Tip into an ice cream maker, add the raspberries and churn according to the manufacturer's instructions. This ice cream can become fairly solid in the freezer, so take it out 20 minutes before serving.

## CHOCOLATE-CHIP ICE CREAM

**SERVES 6–8**

100 G (3½ OZ) CASTER (SUPERFINE) SUGAR
4 EGG YOLKS
250 ML (9 FL OZ/1 CUP) MILK
150 ML (5 FL OZ) CREAM
1 TEASPOON VANILLA EXTRACT OR VANILLA BEAN PASTE
180 G (6 OZ) GOOD-QUALITY DARK CHOCOLATE, FINELY CHOPPED

Whisk the caster sugar and egg yolks together until thick and pale. Stir in the milk, cream and vanilla until well mixed.

Tip the mixture into an ice cream maker and churn according to the manufacturer's instructions. Once churned, stir in the chopped chocolate and serve immediately.

## COCONUT ICE CREAM

SERVES 6

435 ML (15 FL OZ/1¾ CUPS) MILK
115 G (4 OZ/½ CUP) CASTER (SUPERFINE) SUGAR
400 ML (14 FL OZ) COCONUT CREAM

Whisk together the milk and sugar until the sugar has dissolved. Add the coconut cream and mix well. Tip into an ice cream maker and churn according to the manufacturer's instructions.

## WATERMELON GRANITA

SERVES 10–12

2 KG (4 LB 8 OZ) SEEDLESS WATERMELON
115 G (4 OZ/½ CUP) CASTER (SUPERFINE) SUGAR
3 TABLESPOONS LIME JUICE

Cut the watermelon flesh into bite-sized chunks and put in zip-lock freezer bags. Freeze for 1–2 hours or until frozen. Put the frozen watermelon in a food processor and mix until completely smooth. Add the sugar and lime juice and process again until completely incorporated.

Transfer the mixture to an airtight container and freeze for at least 3–4 hours or until firm. Once frozen, scrape the watermelon granita into crystals with a fork and serve immediately.

"Home-made ice creams are always best when they're freshly churned. We just finish the lot and don't bother saving any for the freezer."

It's autumn, and the air starts **harvest** to chill, the leaves dry and fall and the earth finally cools after the long Australian summer. Time slows down and sends me home a bit earlier. A softness starts to creep into the flavours and textures of food and my oven is turned on again.

There is definitely a nostalgia around harvest time that reminds me of my childhood. Presumably because harvest is a much more important signpost of the changing seasons in country Victoria than in busy-busy city Sydney. I would spend most autumn holidays at my uncle's farm, where I was allowed to ride around on the back of the tractor throwing hay to the cattle. We'd trudge back to the farmhouse in the late afternoon gloom and my aunt would've set the table with some hot soup and home-made bread, or her very special melting moments with warm milk.

I loved to pick apples as a child; hundreds of them. This was when I really started to take an interest in cooking: we had apple trees on our farm and my best friend and I would spend most autumn days chopping up apples and 'baking' mud pies in our tree house. The apple-and-mud pie is presumably my first real recipe! Thinking about it now, I know one of my daughters would be in heaven making her own mud pies. I must resurrect that pastime.

A few years ago we found ourselves at a harvest festival in the Barossa Valley, South Australia. A crisp morning with hot mugs of tea and bacon and egg rolls gave us a glorious golden day. The children played on rope swings hanging from the branches of enormous trees and ate popcorn and other fete favourites. Scarecrows peered from every secret spot, scary but intriguing. Leaves in all shades from yellow to ochre to russet were piled high in the grounds of this beautiful old family-owned winery complete with rambling stone homestead. It was one of my very favourite holidays.

Two years later, and we were eating slow-cooked pork shoulder and the local 'bullboar' sausages in the Swiss-Italian settled area of Victoria, where European-style villas and mineral spas are found among gums. We ate on a heated terrace with the wood-fired ovens a few steps away, the llamas a little further, past them the fields of pruned lavender and, on from there, families playing bocce.

Some of my favourite foods are autumnal: roast pork and duck, apples, pears and quinces, pumpkins and mushrooms. Most are best ever-so-slowly cooked. Just as the light becomes softer in autumn, there is a mellowness to what I like to eat, a gentleness of flavours, a sweetness and a hint of spices, rather than the citrus zing of summer. It seems to me such a natural progression of the seasons that the autumn foods take a little longer to prepare and cook, filling the kitchen with warmth and great smells while they do so. It's the earth's way of telling us to warm up and hunker down.

# FROSTY MORNING BREAKFASTS

## BACON AND EGG ROLLS WITH SPICY TOMATO RELISH

**SERVES 4**

4 LARGE BACON RASHERS, HALVED
4 EGGS
125 ML (4 FL OZ/½ CUP) CREAM
A PINCH OF SALT
1 TABLESPOON BUTTER

**TO SERVE**
4 SOFT BREAD ROLLS
ROCKET (ARUGULA)
SPICY TOMATO RELISH, OPPOSITE

Preheat the oven to 200°C (400°F/Gas 6). Line a large baking tray with baking paper, put the bacon on the tray and bake for 10 minutes, or until crisp. Drain on kitchen paper.

Meanwhile, whisk together the eggs, cream and salt. Melt the butter in a non-stick frying pan over high heat, taking care not to let it burn. Pour in the eggs and cook for 20 seconds, or until just set around the edge. With a wooden spoon, gently bring the egg from the outside of the pan to the centre — the idea is to 'fold' rather than scramble the eggs. Leave them to cook for another 20 seconds, then 'fold' again in the same way. When the eggs are just set (remembering that they will continue cooking as they rest) remove from the heat.

Put a couple of pieces of bacon in each roll and top with some egg, rocket leaves and a spoonful of tomato relish.

## SPICY TOMATO RELISH

2 TABLESPOONS OLIVE OIL
1 ONION, FINELY CHOPPED
2 GARLIC CLOVES, THINLY SLICED
1 RED CAPSICUM (PEPPER), SEEDED AND FINELY DICED
1 GREEN CAPSICUM (PEPPER), SEEDED AND FINELY DICED
¼ TEASPOON CAYENNE PEPPER
1 TEASPOON PAPRIKA
1 RED CHILLI, SEEDED AND FINELY CHOPPED
2 TEASPOONS TOMATO PASTE
A PINCH OF SUGAR
1 BAY LEAF
400 G (14 OZ) TIN CHOPPED TOMATOES
SEA SALT
FRESHLY GROUND BLACK PEPPER

Heat the olive oil in a large saucepan over medium-low heat. Add the onion and cook, stirring occasionally, for 5 minutes or until soft. Add the garlic and cook, stirring, for another 2–3 minutes.

Add the capsicums and cook, stirring occasionally, for 10 minutes or until soft. Add the spices, chilli and tomato paste and cook, stirring, for 5 minutes. Add the sugar, bay leaf and tomatoes, bring to a low simmer and simmer for 40 minutes. Season to taste with salt and pepper before serving.

"This relish is great with bacon and egg rolls, but also with roast or cold meats, or sausage rolls. Keep the left-overs in a jar in the fridge."

# PORK, VEAL AND PISTACHIO SAUSAGE ROLLS

**MAKES 16**

1 TABLESPOON OLIVE OIL
1 LARGE ONION, FINELY CHOPPED
2 GARLIC CLOVES, CRUSHED
2 TEASPOONS GROUND CUMIN
1 TEASPOON GROUND CORIANDER
500 G (1 LB 2 OZ) MINCED (GROUND) VEAL
500 G (1 LB 2 OZ) MINCED (GROUND) PORK
70 G (2½ OZ/½ CUP) ROUGHLY CHOPPED PISTACHIO NUTS
1 EGG, PLUS 2 EGG YOLKS
SEA SALT
FRESHLY GROUND BLACK PEPPER
4 SHEETS PUFF PASTRY
2 TABLESPOONS MILK
SESAME SEEDS, TO SPRINKLE

Preheat the oven to 200°C (400°F/Gas 6) and line a large baking tray with baking paper.

Heat the olive oil in a frying pan over medium heat. Add the onion and cook, stirring occasionally, for 5–6 minutes until softened. Add the garlic and spices and cook, stirring, for another minute. Set aside to cool, then tip into a large bowl. Add the veal and pork, pistachios and egg and mix with your hands until thoroughly combined. Season with sea salt and freshly ground black pepper.

Cut each pastry sheet in half, so you have 8 pieces. Working with one piece of pastry at a time, spread an eighth of the filling down the middle of the pastry in a log shape.

Mix together the extra egg yolks and milk and brush around the outside edges of each piece of pastry. Roll up and cut each roll into two pieces. Place on the baking tray with the sealed edges underneath.

Brush the tops of the sausage rolls with the egg wash and sprinkle with sesame seeds. Bake for 25–30 minutes or until golden brown.

## CRUNCHY-TOP PEAR MUFFINS

**MAKES 6**

125 G (4½ OZ/1 CUP) PLAIN (ALL-PURPOSE) FLOUR
60 G (2 OZ/½ CUP) WHOLEMEAL PLAIN (ALL-PURPOSE) FLOUR
3 TEASPOONS BAKING POWDER
2 TEASPOONS GROUND CINNAMON
100 G (3½ OZ/1 CUP) ROLLED OATS
140 G (5 OZ/¾ CUP) BROWN SUGAR
2 EGGS
250 ML (9 FL OZ/1 CUP) PLAIN LOW-FAT YOGHURT
125 ML (4 FL OZ/½ CUP) GRAPESEED OIL (OR OTHER LIGHT-FLAVOURED OIL)
1 PEAR, PEELED AND DICED
40 G (1½ OZ/⅓ CUP) PECAN NUTS, FINELY CHOPPED

Preheat the oven to 180°C (350°F/Gas 4) and line six 250 ml (9 fl oz/1 cup) muffin holes with paper cases (or just grease well). Sift the flours, baking powder and cinnamon into a large bowl, add the oats and ½ cup of the brown sugar and stir together. Make a well in the centre.

Whisk together the eggs, yoghurt and oil. Pour into the well in the dry ingredients and stir until just combined. Fold through the pear, being careful not to overmix. Spoon into the muffin cases.

To make the crumble topping, mix the pecans with the remaining brown sugar. Sprinkle over the muffin mixture and then bake for 20–25 minutes until golden brown.

## PUFFED APPLE PANCAKE

**SERVES 4**

50 G (1¾ OZ) BUTTER
4 TART GREEN APPLES, SUCH AS GRANNY SMITHS, PEELED, CORED AND CUT INTO EIGHTHS
3 TABLESPOONS BROWN SUGAR
1 TEASPOON VANILLA EXTRACT
1 TABLESPOON LEMON JUICE
90 G (3 OZ/¾ CUP) PLAIN (ALL-PURPOSE) FLOUR
A PINCH OF SALT
1 TEASPOON FINELY GRATED LEMON ZEST
1 TABLESPOON SUGAR
4 EGGS
185 ML (6 FL OZ/¾ CUP) MILK

**TO SERVE**
THICK PLAIN YOGHURT WITH A SWIRL OF HONEY OR MAPLE SYRUP

Preheat the oven to 220°C (425°F/Gas 7). Melt the butter in a 25 cm (10 inch) frying pan with an ovenproof handle. Add the apples and cook for 5 minutes over medium heat. Add the brown sugar, vanilla and lemon juice and cook, shaking the pan occasionally, until the sugar has dissolved.

Mix the flour, salt, lemon zest and sugar together in a large bowl, make a well in the centre and slowly add the eggs and milk, whisking lightly to combine (don't worry too much about lumps). Pour the batter evenly over the apples (it's fine if the apples show through). Put the pan in the oven and cook for 15 minutes until puffed and golden. If your pan is shallow, place a baking tray underneath to catch any drips. Serve absolutely immediately, with yoghurt.

"This is a real stick-to-your-ribs breakfast (a bit more like a pudding than a pancake). It's also fabulous with peaches – particularly in late summer when they're so plentiful and cheap."

# RUG-UP-WARM SOUPS

## BARLEY, BEAN AND VEGETABLE SOUP

**SERVES 4**

115 G (4 OZ/½ CUP) BARLEY
2 TABLESPOONS OLIVE OIL
1 ONION, DICED
2 ZUCCHINI (COURGETTES), DICED
2 RED POTATOES, PEELED AND DICED
2 GARLIC CLOVES, CRUSHED
1 BUNCH SILVERBEET (ABOUT 700 G/1 LB 9 OZ), FINELY SHREDDED
1 LITRE (35 FL OZ/4 CUPS) CHICKEN OR VEGETABLE STOCK
400 G (14 OZ) TIN CANNELLINI BEANS, RINSED
200 G (7 OZ) GREEN BEANS, TOPPED AND CUT INTO SHORT LENGTHS
85 G (3 OZ/½ CUP) PEAS (FRESH OR FROZEN)
SEA SALT
FRESHLY GROUND BLACK PEPPER

**TO SERVE**
GRATED PARMESAN

Put the barley in a large saucepan, cover with cold water and bring to the boil. Reduce the heat and simmer for 45 minutes, or until the barley is tender. Rinse under cold running water, drain well and set aside.

Heat the olive oil in a large heavy-based saucepan over medium heat. Add the onion and cook, stirring occasionally, for 5 minutes. Add the zucchini, potato, garlic and silverbeet and cook, stirring occasionally, for 5 minutes more until the silverbeet has wilted.

Add the stock and 1 litre (35 fl oz/4 cups) of water and bring to the boil. Reduce the heat to low and simmer for 20 minutes. Add the cannellini beans and simmer for another 20 minutes. Add the barley, beans and peas and simmer for 5–10 minutes until the vegetables are tender. Season with salt and pepper and grate parmesan over the top to serve.

# WHITE BEAN SOUP WITH BAY AND PANCETTA

**SERVES 4**

2 TABLESPOONS OLIVE OIL
1 TABLESPOON BUTTER
2 ONIONS, CHOPPED
1 TEASPOON SEA SALT
2 BAY LEAVES (FRESH OR DRY)
3 X 400 G (14 OZ) TINS CANNELLINI BEANS, DRAINED
1 LITRE (35 FL OZ/4 CUPS) CHICKEN STOCK

**TO SERVE**
EXTRA VIRGIN OLIVE OIL
50 G (1¾ OZ) PANCETTA, CUT INTO THIN STRIPS AND PAN-FRIED UNTIL CRISP

Put the olive oil and butter in a large saucepan over medium heat. When the butter has melted, add the onion, salt and bay leaves and and cook until the onion is soft and translucent. Add the cannellini beans and chicken stock and bring to the boil, then reduce the heat and simmer for 10 minutes.

Remove the bay leaves and purée the soup in a blender until smooth. Ladle into bowls, drizzle with extra virgin olive oil and top with crisp pancetta to serve.

## CURRIED PARSNIP SOUP WITH CREAM CHEESE TOASTS

SERVES 6

1 TABLESPOON GRAPESEED OIL (OR OTHER LIGHT-FLAVOURED OIL)
2 ONIONS, CHOPPED
3 TABLESPOONS GOOD-QUALITY KORMA CURRY PASTE
1.25 KG (2 LB 12 OZ) PARSNIPS, PEELED AND ROUGHLY CHOPPED
1.5 LITRES (52 FL OZ/6 CUPS) HOT CHICKEN OR VEGETABLE STOCK
150 ML (5 FL OZ) COCONUT MILK
2 TABLESPOONS CHOPPED FRESH CORIANDER (CILANTRO)
SEA SALT
FRESHLY GROUND BLACK PEPPER

TO SERVE
A LITTLE EXTRA COCONUT MILK
CREAM CHEESE TOASTS, BELOW

Heat the oil in a large heavy-based saucepan over medium heat. Add the onion and cook, stirring occasionally, for 5–6 minutes until the onion is soft. Add the curry paste and cook, stirring constantly, for 1–2 minutes until fragrant. Add the parsnips and hot stock and bring to the boil. Reduce the heat to low, cover and simmer for 20 minutes, or until the parsnips are tender. Leave to cool slightly.

Blend the soup in batches until smooth. Return to a clean saucepan and add the coconut milk. Stir over low heat until heated through, then stir through the coriander and season to taste. Serve drizzled with a little extra coconut milk, with a cream cheese toast on the side.

## CREAM CHEESE TOASTS

6 LONG THIN SLICES OF BAGUETTE
100 G (3½ OZ) CREAM CHEESE (FROMAGE BLANC WOULD BE DELICIOUS)

Toast the baguette slices and spread with cream cheese. Serve with curried parsnip soup.

"This makes a great starter for a frosty Northern Hemisphere Christmas dinner."

# HARVEST SUPPERS

## DUCK CASSEROLE WITH GREEN OLIVES AND ORANGE GREMOLATA

**SERVES 4 WITH LEFTOVERS**

8 DUCK MARYLANDS (LEG WITH THIGH)
SEA SALT
FRESHLY GROUND BLACK PEPPER
2 TEASPOONS OLIVE OIL
150 G (5½ OZ) PANCETTA, DICED
1 ONION, FINELY CHOPPED
2 CELERY STALKS, DICED
1 CARROT, DICED
2 GARLIC CLOVES, VERY THINLY SLICED
2 TEASPOONS FENNEL SEEDS, LIGHTLY CRUSHED
250 ML (9 FL OZ/1 CUP) WHITE WINE
400 G (14 OZ) TIN CHOPPED TOMATOES
500 ML (17 FL OZ/2 CUPS) CHICKEN STOCK
175 G (6 OZ/1 CUP) PITTED LARGE GREEN OLIVES

**ORANGE GREMOLATA**
2 TABLESPOONS CHOPPED FRESH FLAT-LEAF (ITALIAN) PARSLEY
2 TEASPOONS FINELY GRATED ORANGE ZEST

Preheat the oven to 220°C (425°F/Gas 7). Put the duck on a large baking tray and season well. Bake for 20–25 minutes until golden brown, then remove. Reduce the oven to 160°C (315°F/Gas 2–3).

Meanwhile, heat the olive oil in a large flameproof casserole over medium heat. Add the pancetta and cook, stirring occasionally, for 5 minutes until crisp. Add the onion, celery, carrot, garlic and fennel seeds and cook, stirring occasionally, for 6–7 minutes until the vegetables are softened. Add the wine and simmer until it has reduced by half. Stir in the tomatoes and chicken stock. Add the browned duck pieces and the olives. Bring to the boil then put the lid on the casserole and cook in the oven for 1½ hours, or until the meat is very tender. Spoon off any excess fat from the surface.

To make the gremolata, mix together the parsley and orange zest. Sprinkle over the casserole and serve with soft polenta.

## SOFT POLENTA

**SERVES 4**

500 ML (17 FL OZ/2 CUPS) SKIM MILK
150 G (5½ OZ/1 CUP) INSTANT POLENTA
3–4 TABLESPOONS GRATED PARMESAN
FRESHLY GROUND BLACK PEPPER

Put the milk and 500 ml (17 fl oz/2 cups) of water in a large saucepan and bring to the boil. Reduce the heat to low and add the polenta in a slow steady stream. Cook for 6–7 minutes, stirring constantly. Remove from the heat, stir in the parmesan and season well with pepper.

## RIGATONI WITH PORK AND FENNEL SAUSAGE

SERVES 4

400 G (14 OZ) RIGATONI
SEA SALT
1 TABLESPOON OLIVE OIL
1 ONION, FINELY CHOPPED
1 CELERY STALK, FINELY CHOPPED
1 GARLIC CLOVE, CRUSHED
2 TEASPOONS CHOPPED FRESH ROSEMARY
500 G (1 LB 2 OZ) PORK AND FENNEL SAUSAGES, CASINGS REMOVED, MEAT CRUMBLED
125 ML (4 FL OZ/½ CUP) CHICKEN STOCK
1 BUNCH ROCKET (ARUGULA), ROUGHLY CHOPPED
FRESHLY GROUND BLACK PEPPER

TO SERVE
GRATED PARMESAN

Cook the rigatoni in a large saucepan of lightly salted boiling water until al dente. Drain well.

Meanwhile, heat the olive oil in a large frying pan over medium heat. Add the onion and celery and cook, stirring occasionally, for 5 minutes or until soft. Add the garlic and rosemary and cook, stirring, for another minute. Add the sausage meat and stir with a wooden spoon to break up the meat. Cook, stirring, for 6–7 minutes until the sausage meat is golden.

Add the chicken stock and simmer for 3–4 minutes until reduced by half. Stir in the rocket and season with black pepper. Toss through the pasta and serve with grated parmesan.

# ROAST CHICKEN WITH CORIANDER CHILLI STUFFING AND COCONUT GRAVY

SERVES 4

3 LARGE HANDFULS CORIANDER (CILANTRO) LEAVES AND STEMS
45 G (1½ OZ/½ CUP) DESICCATED COCONUT
4 LONG GREEN CHILLIES, SEEDED AND ROUGHLY CHOPPED
4 GARLIC CLOVES, CHOPPED
2 TEASPOONS GRATED FRESH GINGER
JUICE OF 2 LIMES
2 TEASPOONS BROWN SUGAR
SEA SALT
FRESHLY GROUND BLACK PEPPER
1 X 1.6 KG (3 LB 8 OZ) FREE-RANGE CHICKEN
2 TABLESPOONS OLIVE OIL

**TO SERVE**
COCONUT GRAVY, BELOW
ROAST POTATOES
STEAMED ASIAN GREENS

To make the stuffing, mix the coriander, coconut, chilli, garlic and ginger in a food processor until finely chopped. Stir in the lime juice and brown sugar and season to taste.

Preheat the oven to 220°C (425°F/Gas 7). Rinse the chicken and pat dry. With your fingers, carefully loosen the skin over the breast of the chicken and down to the thigh area. Push half the stuffing under the skin, spreading it to cover the breast and thigh. Put the remaining stuffing inside the cavity of the chicken. Tie the legs together with kitchen string.

Put the chicken, breast side up, in a large roasting tin, drizzle with olive oil and season with salt and pepper. Roast for 20 minutes, then reduce the oven to 200°C (400°F/Gas 6) and roast for another 50 minutes, or until the juices run clear when you prick the thickest part of the thigh (cover the chicken with foil if it's browning too quickly). Let the chicken rest for 10 minutes before carving. Serve with coconut gravy, roast potatoes and steamed greens.


## COCONUT GRAVY

1 TABLESPOON GREEN CURRY PASTE
250 ML (9 FL OZ/1 CUP) LIGHT COCONUT MILK
1 TABLESPOON LIME JUICE
2 TEASPOONS FISH SAUCE
1 TEASPOON BROWN SUGAR

Heat a small saucepan over medium heat. Add the curry paste and cook, stirring, for 2 minutes or until fragrant. Stir in the coconut milk and simmer for 2–3 minutes. Stir in the lime juice, fish sauce and brown sugar and serve with the chicken and stuffing.

# ROAST CHICKEN WITH TORN BREAD STUFFING AND ONION GRAVY

**SERVES 4**

4 SLICES BREAD (I LIKE TO USE SOY AND LINSEED), CRUSTS REMOVED
1 TABLESPOON OLIVE OIL
1 ONION, FINELY CHOPPED
150 G (5½ OZ/2 CUPS) CHOPPED MUSHROOMS
SEA SALT
FRESHLY GROUND BLACK PEPPER
1 TEAPOON GRATED LEMON ZEST
1 TABLESPOON CHOPPED FRESH SAGE
1 EGG, LIGHTLY BEATEN
1 X 1.6 KG (3 LB 8 OZ) FREE-RANGE CHICKEN

**ONION GRAVY**
1 TABLESPOON BUTTER
2 SMALL ONIONS OR 1 LARGE ONION, FINELY DICED
1½ TABLESPOONS PLAIN (ALL-PURPOSE) FLOUR
500 ML (17 FL OZ/2 CUPS) HOT CHICKEN STOCK
2 TABLESPOONS CREAM

**TO SERVE**
TOMATO AND ZUCCHINI GRATIN, OVERLEAF
APPLE, CELERY AND CUCUMBER SALAD, OVERLEAF

Use your hands to roughly crumble the bread into a large bowl. Put the oil and onion in a frying pan over medium heat and cook for 5 minutes, or until soft. Add the mushrooms and cook for 2 minutes. Transfer to the bowl with the breadcrumbs. Season with salt and pepper, then add the lemon zest, sage and egg, and mix together well. Leave to cool completely.

Preheat the oven to 220°C (425°F/Gas 7). Stuff the chicken cavity with the cold stuffing, then truss by tying the chicken legs together with kitchen string. Roast, breast-up, for 15 minutes, then reduce the oven temperature to 180°C (350°F/Gas 4) and roast for another 45 minutes, or until the juices run clear when you stick a skewer into the thickest part of the thigh. When the chicken is cooked, turn off the oven, leaving the chicken inside, and leave the oven door ajar for 5 minutes for the chicken to rest before carving.

Meanwhile, about 20 minutes before the chicken is ready, make the gravy. Heat a frying pan or saucepan over medium-low heat. Add the butter and onions and cook for 10 minutes until golden brown and caramelised. Add the flour and cook, stirring, for 1–2 minutes until thick. Add the stock and simmer, stirring, until the gravy has thickened. Season to taste and stir in the cream. When the chicken is ready and rested, pour any pan juices into the gravy. (I make gravy in advance to given myself time at the end. Reheat the gravy just before serving, adding more stock or water if it has become too thick.) Serve with tomato and zucchini gratin and apple, celery and cucumber salad.

## TOMATO AND ZUCCHINI GRATIN

**SERVES 4–6**

6 ROMA TOMATOES (ABOUT 800 G/1 LB 12 OZ)
6 ZUCCHINI (COURGETTES) (ABOUT 800 G/1 LB 12 OZ)
1 WHITE ONION
SEA SALT
FRESHLY GROUND BLACK PEPPER
2 GARLIC CLOVES, THINLY SLICED
2 TEASPOONS CHOPPED FRESH THYME
3 LARGE POTATOES, THINLY SLICED
1 TABLESPOON OLIVE OIL

Preheat the oven to 180°C (350°F/Gas 4). Lightly oil a 2 litre (70 fl oz/8 cup) ovenproof dish. Slice the tomatoes vertically, about 5 mm (¼ inch) thick. Slice the zucchini to the same thickness and slice the onion into rounds. Layer the vegetables alternately in the dish, seasoning between the layers with salt and pepper. Scatter the top with the garlic, sprinkle with half the thyme and season again.

Arrange the potatoes, slightly overlapping, in a layer on top of the other vegetables. Sprinkle with the remaining thyme, season again and drizzle with the oil. Bake for 1 hour 15 minutes and then leave to stand for 10 minutes before serving. Great with roast chicken, or any other roast.

## APPLE, CELERY AND CUCUMBER SALAD

**SERVES 4**

2 LEBANESE CUCUMBERS, PEELED AND SEEDED
4 CELERY STALKS
1 APPLE, PEELED AND CUT INTO ROUNDS
A HANDFUL OF LEAVES FROM THE CELERY HEART
SEA SALT
FRESHLY GROUND BLACK PEPPER
1 TABLESPOON LEMON JUICE
1 TABLESPOON EXTRA VIRGIN OLIVE OIL

Cut the cucumbers and celery into thin batons and toss in a bowl with the apple slices and celery leaves. Season with salt and pepper. Whisk together the lemon juice and olive oil, add to the salad and toss together gently.

## CRISP PORK BELLY WITH CARAMEL VINEGAR

SERVES 6

1.5 KG (3 LB 5 OZ) PORK BELLY
2 TABLESPOONS SEA SALT
OLIVE OIL
FRESHLY GROUND BLACK PEPPER

TO SERVE
CARAMEL VINEGAR, OPPOSITE
STEAMED RICE
BOK CHOY WITH SWEET SOY AND LIME, OPPOSITE
FRESHLY CHOPPED RED CHILLI

Score the skin of the pork belly in a criss-cross pattern with a sharp knife. Rub the sea salt into the pork skin and set aside for 30 minutes.

Preheat the oven to 220°C (425°F/Gas 7). Wipe the salt off the pork skin with kitchen paper and dry well. Drizzle a large roasting tin with olive oil. Put the pork belly in the tin skin side down, drizzle with a little more oil and season with salt and pepper.

Roast the pork in the oven for 30 minutes. Reduce the oven temperature to 190°C (375°F/Gas 5) and roast for another 1½ hours. Carefully turn the pork over and roast for another 20 minutes, or until the skin is crisp.

Remove the pork from the oven, cover loosely with foil and set aside to rest for at least 15 minutes. Slice the pork and drizzle with the caramel vinegar. Serve with steamed rice, bok choy with sweet soy and lime, and some freshly chopped red chilli.

"A little chef's trick here: a Stanley knife is the best tool for scoring pork belly."

## CARAMEL VINEGAR

**SERVES 6**

115 G (4 OZ/½ CUP) BROWN SUGAR
80 ML (2¾ FL OZ/⅓ CUP) RED WINE VINEGAR
2 STAR ANISE
1 CINNAMON STICK
250 ML (9 FL OZ/1 CUP) CHICKEN STOCK
JUICE OF 1 ORANGE AND 4 WIDE STRIPS OF ORANGE PEEL
SEA SALT
FRESHLY GROUND BLACK PEPPER

Put the sugar, vinegar, star anise and cinnamon in a small saucepan and cook, stirring, over medium heat until the sugar has dissolved. Bring to the boil and simmer for 5 minutes, or until syrupy.

Stir in the chicken stock and simmer for another 5 minutes, or until slightly reduced. Add the orange juice and peel, reduce the heat to low and simmer gently until thick and syrupy. Season to taste.

## BOK CHOY WITH SWEET SOY AND LIME

**SERVES 6**

125 ML (4 FL OZ/½ CUP) SOY SAUCE
1½ TABLESPOONS CASTER (SUPERFINE) SUGAR
1½ TABLESPOONS LIME JUICE
3 BUNCHES BABY BOK CHOY (PAK CHOY)

Put the soy sauce and sugar in a small saucepan over low heat and stir to dissolve the sugar. Simmer until the soy sauce has reduced by half. Remove from the heat and stir in the lime juice.

Blanch or steam the bok choy until it is bright green and tender crisp. Drizzle with the sweet soy and lime and serve immediately.

"I love the way this caramel vinegar and the hint of lime in the greens cut through the richness of the pork belly."

# PORK MEATBALLS WITH CURRY SAUCE

SERVES 4–6

**MEATBALLS**
600 G (1 LB 5 OZ) MINCED (GROUND) PORK
1 ONION, GRATED
1 EGG, LIGHTLY BEATEN
55 G (2 OZ/⅔ CUP) FRESH WHITE BREADCRUMBS
1 LONG RED CHILLI, SEEDED AND FINELY CHOPPED
2 TEASPOONS GRATED FRESH GINGER
1 TEASPOON GARAM MASALA
2 TABLESPOONS CHOPPED FRESH CORIANDER (CILANTRO)
SEA SALT
FRESHLY GROUND BLACK PEPPER
1 TABLESPOON GRAPESEED OIL (OR OTHER LIGHT-FLAVOURED OIL)

**CURRY SAUCE**
3 TABLESPOONS MASSAMAN CURRY PASTE
2 TEASPOONS GRATED FRESH GINGER
4 TOMATOES, CHOPPED
200 ML (7 FL OZ) COCONUT MILK
200 ML (7 FL OZ) CHICKEN STOCK
1 TABLESPOON LEMON JUICE
2 TEASPOONS BROWN SUGAR

**TO SERVE**
3–4 TABLESPOONS CASHEW NUTS, LIGHTLY TOASTED AND FINELY CHOPPED
2 TABLESPOONS CHOPPED FRESH CORIANDER (CILANTRO)
STEAMED RICE

Preheat the oven to 220°C (425°F/Gas 7). To make the meatballs, put all the ingredients except the oil in a large mixing bowl and mix together well with your hands. Shape into small balls (I find that wetting my hands first makes this easier).

Put the meatballs in a large roasting tin, drizzle with the oil and then toss gently. Bake in the oven for 15–20 minutes, or until golden.

Meanwhile to make the curry sauce, heat a large frying pan over medium heat. Add the curry paste and ginger and cook, stirring, for 1 minute. Add the tomatoes and cook, stirring occasionally, for another 2–3 minutes. Add the coconut milk and stock and bring to the boil. Reduce the heat to low and leave to simmer for 5 minutes. Add the meatballs, stir carefully to coat and then simmer in the sauce for 20 minutes. Gently stir in the lemon juice and brown sugar. Garnish with the cashew nuts and coriander and serve over steamed rice.

## VEAL WITH BALSAMIC, PINE NUTS AND CURRANTS

SERVES 4

4 VEAL SCALLOPINI
2 TABLESPOONS OLIVE OIL
SEA SALT
FRESHLY GROUND BLACK PEPPER
2 TABLESPOONS BALSAMIC VINEGAR
185 ML (6 FL OZ/¾ CUP) CHICKEN OR VEAL STOCK
1 TEASPOON CASTER (SUPERFINE) SUGAR
20 G (1 OZ) CHILLED BUTTER, DICED
2 TABLESPOONS TOASTED PINE NUTS
2 TABLESPOONS CURRANTS, SOAKED IN WARM WATER FOR 5 MINUTES

TO SERVE
CHOPPED FRESH FLAT-LEAF (ITALIAN) PARSLEY
ROCKET AND PUMPKIN SALAD, BELOW

Put the veal scallopini between two pieces of plastic wrap and flatten with a rolling pin until they are thin. Coat all over with olive oil and season with salt and pepper. Heat a large frying pan over medium–high heat and cook the veal, in batches if necessary, for 2 minutes, then turn and cook for 1 minute on the other side. Lift out onto a warm plate and cover with foil.

Add the balsamic vinegar, stock and sugar to the frying pan. Bring to the boil, then turn the heat to medium–low and simmer for 2–3 minutes. Whisk in the butter, piece by piece, then add the pine nuts and drained currants. Pour over the veal and serve sprinkled with parsley.

## ROCKET AND PUMPKIN SALAD

SERVES 4

500 G (1 LB 2 OZ) PUMPKIN, PEELED AND DICED
1 RED ONION, DICED
1 TEASPOON DRIED CHILLI, OR TO TASTE
2 TABLESPOONS OLIVE OIL
SEA SALT
100 G (3½ OZ) ROCKET (ARUGULA)
BALSAMIC VINEGAR, TO DRIZZLE

Preheat the oven to 200°C (400°F/Gas 6). Put the pumpkin, onion, dried chilli, olive oil and salt in a baking dish and toss together. Bake for 20 minutes, or until the pumpkin is browned.

Toss the cooked pumpkin gently with the rocket and drizzle with balsamic vinegar to serve.

# AUTUMN FETE

## CARAMEL POPCORN

**MAKES ABOUT 10 CUPFULS**

75 G (2½ OZ) POPPING CORN
200 ML (7 FL OZ) SWEETENED CONDENSED MILK
110 G (3¾ OZ/½ CUP) BROWN SUGAR
110 G (3¾ OZ/½ CUP) CASTER (SUPERFINE) SUGAR
80 G (2¾ OZ) UNSALTED BUTTER

Pop the corn in a pan or in the microwave, following the instructions on the packet. This should make about 10 cupfuls of popcorn. Preheat the oven to 170°C (325°F/Gas 3). Put the popcorn in a large heatproof bowl and line 2 large baking trays with baking paper.

Put the condensed milk, brown sugar, caster sugar and butter in a saucepan over low heat and stir until the sugar has dissolved. Bring to the boil, reduce the heat and simmer for 1 minute to make caramel. Pour over the popcorn and use a wooden spoon to stir until all the popcorn is completely covered with the caramel.

Spread the popcorn onto the baking trays. Put the trays in the oven and bake for 10–12 minutes, or the popcorn is until golden brown, stirring it occasionally to break up the clumps. Allow to cool completely on the trays before serving.

# COCONUT MARSHMALLOWS

**MAKES 40 PIECES**

**500 G (1 LB 2 OZ) CASTER (SUPERFINE) SUGAR**
**1 TABLESPOON GLUCOSE SYRUP**
**30 G (1 OZ) POWDERED GELATINE**
**2 EGG WHITES**
**1 TEASPOON VANILLA EXTRACT**
**ICING (CONFECTIONER'S) SUGAR, TO DUST**
**TOASTED SHREDDED COCONUT, TO COAT**

Put the sugar, glucose syrup and 210 ml (7½ fl oz) of water in a large saucepan. Stir over low heat until the sugar dissolves. Bring to the boil and boil until the syrup reaches 142°C (275°F) on a sugar thermometer (this is called soft crack stage) — brush down the side of the saucepan with a wet pastry brush if any sugar crystals form. If you don't have a sugar thermometer, you can test the syrup by dropping a small teaspoonful into a bowl of iced water: it has reached soft crack stage when you are able to lift out the ball of syrup and stretch it between your fingers into pliable strands.

Meanwhile, put 140 ml (4½ fl oz) of water in a small heatproof bowl, sprinkle with the gelatine and then place the bowl over a small pan of boiling water until the gelatine has dissolved. Add the gelatine to the cooked sugar syrup (the mixture will initially bubble vigorously).

Meanwhile, beat the egg whites with electric beaters until stiff peaks form. With the beaters running, gradually add the boiling sugar syrup to the egg whites in a thin stream. Continue beating for 7–8 minutes (marshmallow would be exhausting to make if you were beating by hand) until the mixture becomes thick and holds its shape. Add the vanilla and beat until well combined.

Lightly oil a 20 x 30 cm (8 x 12 inch) baking tin and dust with icing sugar. Spread the marshmallow mixture evenly into the tin and smooth the top. Sprinkle with the coconut, pressing it gently into the marshmallow so that it sticks. Leave overnight, or until set. Turn out of the tin and cut into squares with a hot wet knife.

## HAZELNUT AND FIG CAKE

125 G (4½ OZ) UNSALTED BUTTER, SOFTENED
150 G (5½ OZ) CASTER (SUPERFINE) SUGAR
75 G (2½ OZ) PLAIN (ALL-PURPOSE) FLOUR
2 TEASPOONS BAKING POWDER
3 EGGS, LIGHTLY BEATEN
100 G (3½ OZ) GROUND HAZELNUTS
50 G (1¾ OZ) HAZELNUTS, CHOPPED INTO SMALL PIECES
8 FRESH FIGS (NOT TOO RIPE), HALVED
2 TABLESPOONS HONEY

Preheat the oven to 180°C (350°F/Gas 4). Cream the butter and sugar in a large mixing bowl until pale and fluffy. Sift together the flour and baking powder. Use a large metal spoon to fold the flour and egg alternately into the creamed mixture. Fold in the ground hazelnuts and then the chopped hazelnuts.

Grease a 20 cm (8 inch) cake tin and line with baking paper, leaving the paper hanging over the sides to help you lift out the cake. Spoon the mixture into the tin. Arrange the figs, cut side up, in a neat layer on top of cake. Bake for 55 minutes to 1 hour, or until a skewer poked into the middle of the cake comes out clean.

Leave to rest in the tin for 10 minutes before turning out. Drizzle honey over the top of cake just before serving. This is lovely both as a cake and as a dessert with lightly whipped cream.

"I love baked and dried figs but, funnily enough, I'm not so keen on eating them fresh. I think it's because when my brother and I were kids on the farm we would spend afternoons pelting each other with overripe fruit."

# GINGER BISCUITS WITH LEMON DRIZZLE ICING

**MAKES ABOUT 20**

250 G (9 OZ/2 CUPS) PLAIN (ALL-PURPOSE) FLOUR
1 TEASPOON BAKING POWDER
A PINCH OF SALT
1 TEASPOON GROUND GINGER
40 G (1½ OZ/⅓ CUP) ICING (CONFECTIONER'S) SUGAR
70 G (2½ OZ/⅓ CUP) CRYSTALLISED GINGER, FINELY CHOPPED
200 G (7½ OZ) UNSALTED BUTTER, MELTED AND COOLED
1 TEASPOON VANILLA EXTRACT

**LEMON DRIZZLE ICING**
125 G (4½ OZ/1 CUP) ICING (CONFECTIONER'S) SUGAR, SIFTED
1 TABLESPOON LEMON JUICE

Preheat the oven to 180°C (350°F/Gas 4) and line 2 baking trays with baking paper.

Sift the flour, baking powder, salt, ground ginger and icing sugar into a large mixing bowl. Add the crystallised ginger and stir it all together. Add the melted butter and vanilla extract and, using a wooden spoon, stir until everything is well combined.

Roll tablespoons of the dough into balls and set out on the baking trays, leaving enough room for the biscuits to spread. Lightly flatten the balls with a fork dipped in flour. Bake for 12–15 minutes until the biscuits are light golden. Leave on a wire rack to cool.

To make the lemon drizzle icing, mix the icing sugar and lemon juice until smooth and glossy. Once the biscuits are completely cool, drizzle them with icing.

Whether it's a partner, friends or our family, when we love someone it's natural to want to nurture them, and that, **honeymoon** for me anyway, means putting together a special meal. The most meaningful conversations of my life always happen over a table of food.

When Natalie and I met, the most obvious thing we had in common was a great passion for food. We had both been infuriating our respective friends for years by taking three hours to decide where to go for dinner, walking into restaurants then walking straight out again, and forcing everyone to drive around for another hour. We finally got together and friends gleefully remarked that we had both found our nemesis. We think nothing of this lengthy procedure, although it grows ever more complicated now there are three new opinions to throw into the mix.

So, when I first invited Nat round for dinner, the pressure was really on. I remember making a huge effort but, of course, running late and not having a lot of time. She loves champagne, so I had a little half-bottle of Veuve Clicquot chilling, which, I suspect, is what won her heart. I made butterflied chicken with (I still don't know what I was thinking!) rum baba for dessert. And I suppose it must've all been OK, because we're still together.

Sitting in bed on a weekend morning, eating chocolate French toast with the one you love sounds like a most romantic start to the day. But, if anyone with an inquiring mind is wondering why all my breakfast-in-bed recipes 'serve four' rather than two, it is worth noting that anything involving chocolate, or breakfast-in-bed for that matter, in our house has to be served for five. The recipes for these, and all the dinner menus, are easily halved or doubled.

I love the intimacy of sharing a plate of food, and Nat and I have enjoyed countless dishes made to be eaten *à deux*: roast Bresse chicken in Paris, banquets in Japan, and rib-eye steak anywhere we can. Like other couples we 'own' restaurants in many places. They're not always special-occasion venues; sometimes they offer an intimacy that comes with bustle and anonymity, or small size with particularly knowing service. But all are perfect honeymoons in their own way: good food in just the right environment for that particular moment. Whenever we go to London, our first dinner is always lobster and chips at the same little restaurant near our hotel. I suppose people might think it's a little strange to go from Sydney, which has some of the best fresh seafood in the world, to eat lobster in London — but that's the thing about stolen moments together, isn't it? They follow the heart, not the head.

# BREAKFAST IN BED

## CHOCOLATE-FILLED FRENCH TOAST

**SERVES 4**

3 EGGS
185 ML (6 FL OZ/¾ CUP) MILK
1 TABLESPOON CASTER (SUPERFINE) SUGAR
A PINCH OF SALT
1 TABLESPOON UNSALTED BUTTER
8 SLICES WHITE BREAD
100 G (3½ OZ) MILK OR DARK CHOCOLATE, CHOPPED

**TO SERVE**
ICING (CONFECTIONER'S) SUGAR

Whisk together the eggs, milk, caster sugar and salt in a flat dish. Heat the butter in a large frying pan over medium heat.

Dip two slices of the bread into the egg mixture, turning them over until they are completely coated. Put them in the frying pan and sprinkle each one with a quarter of the chopped chocolate. Soak another two slices of bread in the egg mixture and put on top of the chocolate bread in the pan to make sandwiches. Press lightly with a spatula to seal the edges.

Cook for 3 minutes each side or until golden brown. Remove from the pan and serve immediately or keep warm while you make the other two sandwiches. Serve dusted with icing sugar.

"This is a do-it-yourself *pain au chocolat*, for when you can't bring yourselves to leave the house."

## BAKED EGGS WITH SPINACH AND PARMESAN

SERVES 4

1 TABLESPOON OLIVE OIL
200 G (7 OZ) BABY SPINACH LEAVES
SEA SALT
FRESHLY GROUND BLACK PEPPER
8 EGGS
4 TABLESPOONS CREAM
4 TABLESPOONS GRATED PARMESAN

**TO SERVE**
TOAST

Preheat the oven to 200°C (400°F/Gas 6). Lightly grease four 9 cm (3½ inch) ramekins and place on a baking tray.

Heat a saucepan or frying pan over medium heat. Add the oil to the pan, then add the spinach and season with salt and pepper. Cook until the leaves are just softened. Drain the spinach in a colander and, as soon as it's cool enough to handle, squeeze out the excess liquid.

Spoon the spinach into the ramekins and break 2 eggs into each ramekin on top of the spinach. Pour 1 tablespoon of cream over the eggs and sprinkle with 1 tablespoon of parmesan. Bake for 15 minutes, or until the eggs are set and puffed up. Season and serve immediately with toast.

"There's an
intimacy about
breakfast
that I think can't
be recaptured
in even the
most expensive
restaurant dinner."

## BLUEBERRY BREAKFAST SCONES

**MAKES 8 WEDGES**

250 G (9 OZ/2 CUPS) PLAIN (ALL-PURPOSE) FLOUR
1 TABLESPOON CASTER (SUPERFINE) SUGAR
3 TEASPOONS BAKING POWDER
A PINCH OF SALT
100 G (3½ OZ) COLD UNSALTED BUTTER, CUBED
2 EGGS, LIGHTLY BEATEN
125 ML (4 FL OZ/½ CUP) CREAM
85 G (3 OZ/½ CUP) BLUEBERRIES, FROZEN OR FRESH, TOSSED IN A LITTLE FLOUR
1 EGG, MIXED WITH 1 TABLESPOON MILK, FOR GLAZING

Preheat the oven to 200°C (400°F/Gas 6) and line a baking tray with baking paper.

Pulse the flour, sugar, baking powder and salt in a food processor until combined. Add the butter and pulse until it is roughly combined (there will still be lumps of butter). Tip into a bowl and mix in the eggs and cream with a knife. Gently mix in the blueberries with your hands (tossing them in a bit of flour first prevents them all sinking to the bottom of the dough).

Turn the dough onto a lightly floured surface and press into a 15 cm (6 inch) square. Cut into quarters and then cut each quarter in half.  Place on the baking tray and brush with the egg and milk glaze. Bake for 15–20 minutes or until golden. Serve warm, with butter if you like.

# DINNER DATES

## DUCK, RADICCHIO AND FIG SALAD

**SERVES 2 COUPLES**

4 DUCK BREASTS WITH SKIN
1 TABLESPOON BROWN SUGAR
1 TEASPOON GROUND CINNAMON
80 ML (2½ FL OZ/⅓ CUP) PINK GRAPEFRUIT JUICE
3 TABLESPOONS CHICKEN STOCK
2 TABLESPOONS REDCURRANT JELLY
1 BUNCH OF ROCKET (ARUGULA), TRIMMED AND ROUGHLY TORN
1 HEAD OF RADICCHIO, TRIMMED AND ROUGHLY TORN
4 RIPE FIGS, QUARTERED
30 G (1 OZ/⅓ CUP) WALNUTS, LIGHTLY TOASTED, ROUGHLY CHOPPED

Preheat the oven to 180°C (350°F/Gas 4). Score the skin on each duck breast 5–6 times. Mix together the brown sugar and cinnamon and rub into the duck skin.

Heat a large frying pan over medium heat and cook the duck, skin side down, for 6–7 minutes until the skin is crisp and the fat has rendered down. Turn over and cook for another minute. Put the duck on a baking tray and bake in the oven for 5 minutes.

To make the dressing, return the frying pan to medium-high heat. Add the grapefruit juice, stock and redcurrant jelly and whisk them together over the heat. Simmer for 3–4 minutes until the dressing has reduced by half.

Slice the duck on the diagonal. Divide the rocket, radicchio and figs among four serving plates. Top with some slices of duck and sprinkle with walnuts. Drizzle with a little of the dressing and serve immediately.

## LEMON PUDDINGS

SERVES 2 COUPLES

3 TABLESPOONS PLAIN (ALL-PURPOSE) FLOUR, SIFTED
80 ML (2½ FL OZ/⅓ CUP) LEMON JUICE
2 TEASPOONS FINELY GRATED LEMON ZEST
4 EGGS, SEPARATED
140 G (5 OZ/⅔ CUP) CASTER (SUPERFINE) SUGAR
200 ML (7 FL OZ) MILK
2 TABLESPOONS BUTTER, MELTED

**TO SERVE**
THICK (DOUBLE) CREAM

Preheat the oven to 180°C (350°F/Gas 4) and lightly grease four 250 ml (9 fl oz/1 cup) ovenproof dishes. Put the flour, lemon juice, lemon zest and egg yolks into a large bowl and add all but 2 tablespoons of the caster sugar. Whisk together well, then add the milk and melted butter and whisk again until well combined.

In another bowl, whisk the egg whites and remaining caster sugar until firm peaks form. Gently fold half the egg white into the lemon mixture with a metal spoon, then fold in the rest. Spoon into the dishes and bake for 15 minutes, or until light golden and set. Serve with thick cream.

"These little puddings are mini bowls of lemon delicious – golden sponge topping a gooey lemon sauce underneath."

# MENU TWO

## CRISPY SKINNED SALMON WITH TAMARIND CARAMEL DRESSING

SERVES 3 COUPLES

800 G (1 LB 12 OZ) SALMON FILLETS WITH SKIN, CUBED, BONES REMOVED
1 TABLESPOON OLIVE OIL
SEA SALT
FRESHLY GROUND BLACK PEPPER
2 BUNCHES OF MIZUNA, LEAVES PICKED (OR 140 G/5 OZ BABY ROCKET/ARUGULA)
2 LEBANESE CUCUMBERS, HALVED AND THINLY SLICED
A HANDFUL OF FRESH CORIANDER (CILANTRO) LEAVES
A HANDFUL OF FRESH MINT LEAVES
TAMARIND CARAMEL DRESSING, BELOW

Heat a frying pan over medium-high heat for 2 minutes. Brush the salmon with oil and season well with salt and pepper. Cook the salmon, skin side down, for 3 minutes, then turn over and cook for another minute. Remove from the pan and leave to rest for 2 minutes. The salmon should be quite rare and the skin crispy.

Toss together the mizuna (or rocket), cucumber, coriander and mint. Arrange the salad on a large serving platter, top with the salmon and drizzle with some of the tamarind caramel dressing.

## TAMARIND CARAMEL DRESSING

1 TEASPOON GRAPESEED OIL (OR OTHER LIGHT-FLAVOURED OIL)
1 TEASPOON FINELY GRATED FRESH GINGER
3 TABLESPOONS LIGHT SOY SAUCE
115 G (4 OZ/$\frac{1}{2}$ CUP) BROWN SUGAR
1 TABLESPOON FISH SAUCE
2 TEASPOONS TAMARIND PUREE

Heat the oil in a small saucepan over medium heat. Add the ginger and stir for 30 seconds. Add the soy sauce and brown sugar and cook, stirring, until the sugar has dissolved. Add the fish sauce and tamarind and cook, stirring, until syrupy. Allow to cool slightly before serving.

## CARAMEL COCONUT PANNACOTTA

**SERVES 3 COUPLES**

**2 SHEETS OF LEAF GELATINE**
**250 ML (9 FL OZ/1 CUP) COCONUT MILK**
**400 ML (14 FL OZ) CREAM**
**70 G (2¹/₂ OZ) CASTER (SUPERFINE) SUGAR**
**¹/₂ VANILLA BEAN, SPLIT**

**CARAMEL**
**175 G (6 OZ/³/₄ CUP) CASTER (SUPERFINE) SUGAR**

To make the caramel, put the sugar and 125 ml (4 fl oz/¹/₂ cup) of water in a saucepan and stir over low heat to dissolve the sugar. Bring to the boil, reduce the heat and simmer without stirring for 6–10 minutes, or until the syrup turns the colour of honey. Remove from the heat and quickly pour the caramel into six 125 ml (4 fl oz/¹/₂ cup) dariole moulds, turning the moulds so the caramel coats the base and sides.

Soak the gelatine in a small bowl of cold water for 5 minutes. Meanwhile, place the coconut milk, cream, sugar and vanilla bean in a small saucepan and stir over low heat until the sugar has dissolved. Bring to a very gentle simmer, then remove from the heat. Squeeze the water out of the softened gelatine, add to the pan and stir until it has dissolved.

Strain the mixture through a fine sieve and pour into the dariole moulds. Refrigerate until set. These will keep very well in the fridge for up to 3 days. To serve, dip each mould into hot water for a few seconds, making sure the water only comes halfway up the side. Hold a plate over the top and invert the pannacotta.

"If you can find them, buy plastic dariole moulds – they're flexible, and much easier to use than the metal ones. Takeaway coffee cups make a great substitute."

# MENU THREE

## JAPANESE TOFU STEAK WITH SESAME

SERVES 2 COUPLES

3 TABLESPOONS LIGHT SOY SAUCE
2–3 TABLESPOONS MIRIN
2 TEASPOONS SESAME OIL
600 G (1 LB 5 OZ) FIRM TOFU, DRAINED
CORNFLOUR (CORNSTARCH), TO DUST
SEA SALT
FRESHLY GROUND BLACK PEPPER
2 TABLESPOONS PEANUT OIL
1 TABLESPOON SESAME SEEDS, LIGHTLY TOASTED

Whisk together the soy sauce, mirin and sesame oil in a bowl. Cut the tofu into eight 1.5 cm (⅝ inch) thick steaks. Sprinkle the cornflour on a large plate and season with sea salt and freshly ground black pepper. Coat each tofu steak in cornflour on both sides.

Heat the peanut oil in a large frying pan over high heat and cook the tofu in batches for 2–3 minutes on each side until golden brown and crisp. Drain on kitchen paper. Drizzle with the sauce and sprinkle with sesame seeds to serve.

## ASPARAGUS AND BABY BEANS WITH CHILLI AND SESAME SEEDS

SERVES 2 COUPLES

2 BUNCHES OF ASPARAGUS, WOODY ENDS TRIMMED
250 G (9 OZ) SMALL GREEN BEANS, TOPPED BUT NOT TAILED
2 TABLESPOONS OLIVE OIL
1 LONG RED CHILLI, SEEDED AND FINELY CHOPPED
2 GARLIC CLOVES, THINLY SLICED
1 TEASPOON SESAME OIL
2 TABLESPOONS SOY SAUCE

Blanch the asparagus and beans in a saucepan of lightly salted boiling water for 1–2 minutes until bright green and tender crisp. Refresh in cold water until completely cool, then drain well. Halve the asparagus lengthways.

Heat the oil in a large wok or frying pan over high heat. Add the chilli and garlic and stir-fry for 30 seconds. Add the vegetables and sesame oil and stir fry for 1–2 minutes until the vegetables are slightly crisp and heated through. Add the soy sauce, heat through and pile onto a serving platter.

# CRISPY CHICKEN WITH PONZU

**SERVES 2 COUPLES**

8 CHICKEN THIGH FILLETS WITH SKIN
SEA SALT
FRESHLY GROUND BLACK PEPPER
2 TABLESPOONS GRAPESEED OIL (OR OTHER LIGHT-FLAVOURED OIL)

**PONZU DRESSING**
3 TABLESPOONS LIME JUICE
3 TABLESPOONS LEMON JUICE
125 ML (4 FL OZ/½ CUP) MIRIN
80 ML (2½ FL OZ/⅓ CUP) LIGHT SOY SAUCE

**TO SERVE**
8 SPRING ONIONS (SCALLIONS), FINELY SLICED
RICE AND WASABI

To make the ponzu dressing, put the lime juice, lemon juice and mirin in a small saucepan. Bring to the boil, simmer for 1 minute and then remove from the heat and leave to cool. Add the soy and stir together well.

Pierce the skin of the chicken several times with a skewer or fork. Season well with sea salt and freshly ground black pepper. Heat the oil in a large frying pan over high heat. Add the chicken, in batches, skin side down, and cook for 2–3 minutes until skin is golden and crisp — if you put a smaller pan on top of the chicken and weight it down with some tins, this will make the chicken skin very crispy. Turn the chicken over, cover the pan with a lid and cook for 2–3 minutes until the chicken is cooked through.

Slice the chicken, arrange on a serving plate, sprinkle with the spring onions and drizzle with the ponzu dressing. Serve with rice and wasabi.

"Japanese food
is just perfect
for romantic
dinners. The
flavours are
clean and light,
without any
of those heavy
sauces that
make you
fall asleep
on the sofa."

## PASSIONFRUIT, RAMBUTAN AND MANGO SALAD

**SERVES 2 COUPLES**

**12 RAMBUTANS OR LYCHEES, PEELED AND SEEDS REMOVED**
**2 MANGOES, CHEEKS SLICED OFF AND SCORED**

**PASSIONFRUIT SYRUP**
**3 TABLESPOONS PASSIONFRUIT PULP**
**JUICE OF 1 ORANGE, STRAINED**
**JUICE OF ½ LEMON, STRAINED**
**85 G (3 OZ/⅓ CUP) CASTER (SUPERFINE) SUGAR**

**TO SERVE**
**FRESH MINT LEAVES**

For the syrup, put the passionfruit pulp in a small pan with the orange and lemon juice and sugar and stir over medium heat until the sugar dissolves. Bring to the boil, then reduce the heat to medium-low and simmer, stirring occasionally, for 10 minutes or until syrupy. Cool completely.

Arrange the rambutans or lychees and mango on a platter. Scatter with mint leaves and drizzle with the passionfruit syrup. Serve immediately.

"If you love the taste of passionfruit but aren't keen on the seeds, give the pulp a quick pulse in a food processor or blender. This loosens the seeds enough for you to strain them out."

# MENU FOUR

## LOBSTER AND EGG NOODLE SALAD WITH ORANGE AND GINGER DRESSING

**SERVES 2 COUPLES**

250 G (9 OZ) EGG NOODLES
2 BUNCHES OF ASPARAGUS, TRIMMED AND CUT INTO SHORT LENGTHS ON THE DIAGONAL
800 G (1 LB 12 OZ) COOKED LOBSTER TAIL, SHELL REMOVED
ORANGE AND GINGER DRESSING, BELOW
3 TABLESPOONS SESAME SEEDS, LIGHTLY TOASTED
4 SPRING ONIONS (SCALLIONS) CUT INTO SHORT LENGTHS ON THE DIAGONAL

Cook the egg noodles in a large pan of lightly salted boiling water following the packet instructions and adding the asparagus for the last 2 minutes of the cooking time. Rinse under cold running water and drain well.

Cut the lobster into medallions. Put the noodles, asparagus and lobster in a large bowl and toss together. Add the orange and ginger dressing and half the sesame seeds and toss to evenly coat the salad. Top with the spring onion and remaining sesame seeds to serve.

## ORANGE AND GINGER DRESSING

2 TABLESPOONS ORANGE JUICE
2 TABLESPOONS MIRIN
1 TABLESPOON LIGHT SOY SAUCE
1 TEASPOON GRATED FRESH GINGER
1 TABLESPOON GRAPESEED OIL (OR OTHER LIGHT-FLAVOURED OIL)
1 TEASPOON SESAME OIL

Stir together the orange juice, mirin, soy and ginger. Slowly whisk in the oils until well combined.

# CHOCOLATE ALMOND CAKES WITH CHOCOLATE LIQUEUR SAUCE

**SERVES 2 COUPLES**

80 G (2¾ OZ) UNSALTED BUTTER
60 G (2¼ OZ) DARK CHOCOLATE, CHOPPED
2 TEASPOONS HONEY
60 G (2¼ OZ/½ CUP) ICING (CONFECTIONER'S) SUGAR
3 TABLESPOONS PLAIN (ALL-PURPOSE) FLOUR
40 G (1½ OZ) ALMOND MEAL (GROUND ALMONDS)
2 EGG WHITES, LIGHTLY WHISKED

**TO SERVE**
CHOCOLATE LIQUEUR SAUCE, BELOW
VANILLA ICE CREAM

Preheat the oven to 180°C (350°F/Gas 4) and grease four 125 ml (4 fl oz/½ cup) muffin moulds.

Place a bowl over a saucepan of barely simmering water. Put the butter, chocolate and honey in the bowl and stir until melted and well combined. Set aside to cool.

Sift the sugar and flour into the bowl of cooled chocolate mixture. Add the almond meal, then add the egg whites and stir together well (at this point you can keep the mixture in the fridge for 30 minutes if helpful). Spoon into the muffin moulds and bake for 15 minutes, or until the surface is firm (the middle will still be runny). Leave to cool for a few minutes before serving with the sauce and ice cream.


# CHOCOLATE LIQUEUR SAUCE

125 ML (4 FL OZ/½ CUP) CREAM
115 G (4 OZ) DARK CHOCOLATE, CHOPPED
2 TABLESPOONS LIQUEUR (A COFFEE-FLAVOURED LIQUEUR WORKS WELL)

Heat the cream in a pan over low heat. Once the cream is warm, add the chocolate and stir until melted. Stir in the liqueur. Allow to cool and thicken.

# MENU FIVE

## LA PLANCHA-STYLE RIB-EYE WITH GARLIC OR HORSERADISH BUTTER

**SERVES 2 COUPLES**

**4 TEASPOONS SEA SALT**
**2 X 400 G (14 OZ) RIB-EYE STEAKS**

**GARLIC BUTTER**
**125 G (4½ OZ) BUTTER, SOFTENED**
**2 GARLIC CLOVES, CRUSHED**
**1 TEASPOON FINELY GRATED LEMON ZEST**
**1 TABLESPOON FINELY CHOPPED FRESH FLAT-LEAF (ITALIAN) PARSLEY**

**HORSERADISH BUTTER**
**125 G (4½ OZ) BUTTER, SOFTENED**
**1 TABLESPOON FINELY GRATED FRESH HORSERADISH**
**1 TEASPOON FINELY GRATED LEMON ZEST**
**1 TABLESPOON FINELY CHOPPED FRESH FLAT-LEAF (ITALIAN) PARSLEY**

Put all the ingredients for the garlic or horseradish butter in a food processor and blend until smooth. Shape into a log on plastic wrap, roll up, seal and chill in the fridge for at least 2 hours.

Heat a large frying pan over high heat and sprinkle the pan with sea salt. When the pan is very hot, add the steak and cook for 4 minutes. Turn the steak and cook for 3 minutes on the other side. Set aside in the pan to rest for 10 minutes. Serve one steak per couple, with slices of garlic or horseradish butter and baked new potatoes.

## BAKED NEW POTATOES ON A BED OF SALT

**SERVES 2 COUPLES**

**SEA SALT**
**750 G (1 LB 10 OZ) NEW POTATOES**

Preheat the oven to 200°C (400°F/Gas 6). Sprinkle the base of a roasting tin with a layer of sea salt and arrange the potatoes on top of the salt. Bake, turning the potatoes once, for 50–60 minutes (depending on their size) or until the potatoes are blistered on the outside and very soft and fluffy inside.

# RASPBERRY SOUFFLES

SERVES 2 COUPLES

MELTED BUTTER AND CASTER (SUPERFINE) SUGAR, TO DUST THE MOULDS
200 G (7 OZ) RASPBERRIES, FRESH OR THAWED FROZEN
115 G (4 OZ/½ CUP) CASTER (SUPERFINE) SUGAR
2 TEASPOONS CORNFLOUR (CORNSTARCH), MIXED WITH 2 TEASPOONS COLD WATER
4 EGG WHITES
ICING (CONFECTIONER'S) SUGAR, TO DUST

Brush the base and sides of four 250 ml (9 fl oz/1 cup) soufflé dishes or coffee cups with melted butter and sprinkle with caster sugar, tipping out the excess. Chill in the fridge for 20 minutes, then repeat. Chill again until you are ready to use.

Process the raspberries in a food processer until smooth, then tip into a small saucepan with half the caster sugar. Stir over low heat until the sugar has dissolved. Bring to the boil and stir in the cornflour mixture. Remove from the heat but continue stirring until it is all well mixed. Leave to cool completely.

Preheat the oven to 170°C (325°F/Gas 3). Beat the egg whites with a pinch of salt until soft peaks form. Gradually add the remaining caster sugar until the mixture is thick and glossy. Add a third of the egg white to the raspberry purée, mixing it in well with a metal spoon, then add the rest of the egg white and gently mix it in. Spoon into the dishes and smooth the tops. Bake for 12–14 minutes, until well risen and starting to colour. Dust with icing sugar and serve immediately.

Food plays such a different role in winter, warming us from the inside when it starts to chill outside. There's something about cold drizzly days, with rain running down the windows, that makes me immediately reach for the fireside roasting tin. And this is definitely the time for puddings.

Although I am most definitely a summer person, and often spend my holidays following the sun, even I can see the appeal of freezing winter breaks where you snuggle down in a little cottage and there's nothing to do but sit by the fire and read a book. Occasionally you venture out for a quick walk in the biting cold, purely as an excuse to hurry home and cook up an enormous warming dinner. I've never been on a skiing holiday, but every winter I think about booking one. So the roasts and stews in this chapter are what I'll be making when I find myself in that little log cabin with the roaring open fire.

As the days get shorter and colder, the way we eat seems to expand and warm in response. The oven and the stove top are busy every evening and the ingredients I use begin to subtly change. I love spices in food all year round, but when the weather turns cold I start to build up the layers to make curries and hot one-pots — great for curling up in an armchair with a bowl and a fork.

I once spent an icy winter in Tokyo where one-bowl meals were a real life-saver. Everywhere was a frantic rush of hurtling trains and fast-moving crowds. I warmed up on beef curries and slurped noodles in food halls, while old women sat around me eating sushi and drinking beer at 10 o'clock in the morning.

Tokyo was definitely cold but the coldest I've ever been was in Amsterdam, and that was sitting inside a restaurant! I'd been touring Amsterdam and Antwerp, eating dense apple cakes and caramel biscuits and steak frites with four different types of mayonnaise. On this particular evening, I went to a satay restaurant where, as the meal progressed, I put my coat back on, then my scarf and finally my hat (I would've put gloves on too, if I'd had them). At last I had to call the shirt-sleeved waiter over and ask if they could put the heating on. It was a great display of Dutch stoicism. Wonderful satay, though.

Winter is the time of year for indulging in baked and sticky puddings of the sort that are best served with a jug of warm custard. When we had our first daughter, Edie, it was August, one of Sydney's coldest months. The thing that both Natalie and I remember most clearly (just about the *only* thing we remember clearly) from those first few blurry weeks of learning how to be parents is a sort of compulsion we both had to stay in the house all day making sticky puddings. We grew fatter and fatter in our little family cocoon until we finally struggled outside again to discover the sun had broken through and winter was coming to an end.

# WINTER ONE-POT SUPPERS

## SOY- AND MIRIN-SIMMERED BEEF ON RICE

**SERVES 4**

150 ML (5 FL OZ) WHITE WINE
100 ML (3½ FL OZ) SOY SAUCE
100 ML (3½ FL OZ) MIRIN
2 CM (¾ INCH) PIECE OF FRESH GINGER, PEELED AND THINLY SLICED
3 TABLESPOONS CASTER (SUPERFINE) SUGAR
1 WHITE ONION, THINLY SLICED
500 G (1 LB 2 OZ) RUMP STEAK, THINLY SLICED

**TO SERVE**
STEAMED JAPANESE RICE
BABY SPINACH LEAVES
PICKLED GINGER OR RADISH

Put the white wine, soy, mirin, ginger, sugar and 100 ml (3½ fl oz) water in a saucepan over medium heat. Cook, stirring to dissolve the sugar, then bring to the boil and simmer for 2–3 minutes.

Add the onion and simmer for 4–5 minutes or until the onion is soft. Add the beef and simmer for a further 1–2 minutes until just cooked through.

To serve, spoon rice and spinach leaves into four serving bowls. Top with the beef and onions and ladle some of the hot broth over the top. Garnish with pickled ginger or radish.

"This was my staple diet as a freezing nineteen-year-old living in Japan. It got me through my first Tokyo winter."

## TOMATO AND PANEER WITH SPINACH AND PEAS

**SERVES 4**

3 TABLESPOONS GRAPESEED OIL (OR OTHER LIGHT-FLAVOURED OIL)
400 G (14 OZ) PANEER, CUT INTO SMALL CUBES
1 LARGE RED ONION, FINELY CHOPPED
2 GARLIC CLOVES, CRUSHED
2 TEASPOONS GRATED FRESH GINGER
1½ TEASPOONS CUMIN SEEDS
3 TEASPOONS GROUND CORIANDER
PINCH OF CAYENNE PEPPER
800 G (1 LB 12 OZ) TINNED CHOPPED TOMATOES
150 G (5½ OZ/1 CUP) PEAS (FROZEN ARE FINE)
100 G (3½ OZ) BABY SPINACH
LIME JUICE AND BROWN SUGAR, TO TASTE

**TO SERVE**
BASMATI RICE
THICK PLAIN YOGHURT

Heat the oil in a large pan over medium-high heat. Fry the cheese in batches until golden brown, then drain on kitchen paper. Pour off the excess oil from the pan, leaving about 1 tablespoon.

Return the pan to medium heat. Add the onion and cook, stirring occasionally, for 5–6 minutes or until the onion is soft. Add the garlic, ginger and spices and cook, stirring, until fragrant. Add the tomatoes and 125 ml (4 fl oz/½ cup) of water and bring to the boil. Reduce the heat and simmer for 15 minutes.

Add the peas and simmer for 3–4 minutes, then add the cheese and simmer until the peas are just cooked through. Remove from the heat, stir through the spinach until just wilted and season to taste with lime juice and brown sugar. Serve with steamed basmati rice and thick plain yoghurt.

"Paneer is an Indian-style soft cheese. If you can't find it (or if you want a great vegan winter supper) use firm tofu instead."

## GINGER AND SESAME RICE WITH POACHED CHICKEN

**SERVES 4**

2 TABLESPOONS PEANUT OIL
1 TABLESPOON SESAME OIL
1 ONION, FINELY CHOPPED
3 GARLIC CLOVES, CRUSHED
1 TABLESPOON GRATED FRESH GINGER
400 G (14 OZ) JASMINE RICE
750 ML (26 FL OZ/3 CUPS) CHICKEN STOCK
500 G (1 LB 2 OZ) CHICKEN BREAST FILLETS, CUT INTO THIN ESCALOPES

**TO SERVE**
FINELY SLICED SPRING ONIONS (SCALLIONS)
CHOPPED RED CHILLI
SOY SAUCE

Heat the peanut oil and sesame oil in a large deep frying pan over medium-low heat. Add the onion and cook, stirring occasionally, for 5–6 minutes until soft. Add the garlic and ginger and cook, stirring, for 2 minutes more.

Add the rice and stir to coat the grains of rice with the oil. Add the stock and bring to the boil. Cover, reduce the heat to low and simmer for 5 minutes. Place the chicken in a single layer on top of the rice. Cover again and simmer for a further 8–10 minutes, or until the rice is just tender and the chicken is cooked through (use your watch and try to resist lifting up the lid to check, because you'll let the heat out).

Remove from the heat and set aside, still with the lid on, for a further 5 minutes. Serve sprinkled with spring onion and chilli and drizzled with soy sauce.

# ROASTS AND STEWS

## SLOW-ROASTED PORK SHOULDER WITH CUMIN AND CORIANDER SEEDS

**SERVES 6**

1 TEASPOON CUMIN SEEDS
1 TEASPOON CORIANDER SEEDS
2 KG (4 LB 8 OZ) PORK SHOULDER ON THE BONE
OLIVE OIL
SEA SALT
FRESHLY GROUND BLACK PEPPER

Preheat the oven to 240°C (475°F/Gas 8). Crush the cumin and coriander seeds with a mortar and pestle (or use the end of a rolling pin). Put the pork in a large roasting tin, drizzle with olive oil and rub with the crushed spices. Season well with sea salt and freshly ground black pepper. Put in the oven and roast for 30 minutes or until the pork is browned, then remove from the oven.

Reduce the oven to 180°C (350°F/Gas 4). Moisten a large piece of baking paper with water and place over the pork, tucking the edges underneath. Return to the oven and roast for 2 hours or until tender. Rest for 10 minutes before carving. Serve with braised potatoes and peppers with bay leaves.

## BRAISED POTATOES AND PEPPERS WITH BAY

**SERVES 6**

3 TABLESPOONS OLIVE OIL
2 RED ONIONS, SLICED
750 G (1 LB 10 OZ) YELLOW WAXY POTATOES (SUCH AS NICOLA), PEELED, CUT INTO WEDGES
1 LARGE RED CAPSICUM (PEPPER), CUT INTO THIN STRIPS
1 LARGE GREEN CAPSICUM (PEPPER), CUT INTO THIN STRIPS
3 GARLIC CLOVES
3 BAY LEAVES
250 ML (9 FL OZ/1 CUP) CHICKEN STOCK
SEA SALT
FRESHLY GROUND BLACK PEPPER

Heat the olive oil in a large non-stick deep frying pan over medium-low heat. Add the onions and cook, stirring occasionally, for 10 minutes. Add the potatoes, capsicums, garlic and bay leaves and cook, stirring occasionally, for another 10 minutes.

Add the stock and bring to the boil. Reduce the heat to low, cover and simmer for 20 minutes. Remove the lid, increase the heat to medium and continue to simmer, stirring occasionally, for 10–20 minutes until all the stock has evaporated and the potatoes are tender, coloured and starting to form a crust. Season well with sea salt and freshly ground black pepper.

## SWEET POTATO AND CHICKPEA TAGINE

**SERVES 4**

2 TABLESPOONS OLIVE OIL
1 LARGE ONION, FINELY CHOPPED
2 GARLIC CLOVES, CRUSHED
2 TEASPOONS GRATED FRESH GINGER
2 TEASPOONS GROUND CUMIN
1 CINNAMON STICK
½ TEASPOON SAFFRON THREADS, SOAKED IN 3 TABLESPOONS COLD WATER
400 ML (14 FL OZ) VEGETABLE STOCK
800 G (1 LB 12 OZ) SWEET POTATOES, PEELED AND CUT INTO SMALL CUBES
400 G (14 OZ) TIN CHICKPEAS, RINSED
200 G (7 OZ) GREEN BEANS, TRIMMED AND CUT INTO SHORT LENGTHS
1 TEASPOON HONEY
SEA SALT
FRESHLY GROUND BLACK PEPPER

**TO SERVE**
COUSCOUS
PLAIN YOGHURT
CHOPPED FRESH CORIANDER (CILANTRO)

Heat the olive oil in a large heavy-based saucepan over medium heat. Add the onion and cook, stirring occasionally, for 5–6 minutes or until the onion is soft. Add the garlic, ginger, cumin and cinnamon and cook, stirring, for 1–2 minutes until fragrant.

Add the saffron threads in their water and the vegetable stock and bring to the boil. Add the sweet potato, reduce the heat, cover and simmer for 15 minutes or until the sweet potato is tender. Add the chickpeas and beans and simmer for 5 minutes, or until beans are bright green and tender. Stir through the honey and season with sea salt and freshly ground black pepper.

Serve the tagine on couscous, topped with some yoghurt and chopped coriander.

"Tagines are usually slow-cooking: this is my speeded-up version."

"The best thing about wintery holidays is that spending time at home pottering in the kitchen all day feels so utterly right."

# BRAISED LAMB SHANKS

**SERVES 4**

8 FRENCH-CUT LAMB SHANKS
PLAIN (ALL-PURPOSE) FLOUR, SEASONED WITH SALT AND PEPPER, TO TOSS
2 TABLESPOONS OLIVE OIL
1 LARGE ONION, CUT INTO THIN WEDGES
3 GARLIC CLOVES, THINLY SLICED
1 LONG RED CHILLI, SEEDED AND FINELY CHOPPED
2 TEASPOONS GRATED FRESH GINGER
1 TEASPOON FIVE SPICE POWDER
400 G (14 OZ) TIN CHOPPED TOMATOES
3 TABLESPOONS LIGHT SOY SAUCE
2 TEASPOONS BROWN SUGAR

**TO SERVE**
STEAMED LEAFY GREENS
STEAMED RICE
LIME WEDGES

Toss the lamb shanks in the seasoned flour, shaking off any excess. Heat 1 tablespoon of the oil in a large heavy-based pan over high heat. Brown the lamb on all sides, in batches, then remove all the lamb from the pan.

Return the pan to medium heat and add the rest of the oil. Add the onion and cook, stirring occasionally, for 2–3 minutes. Add the garlic, chilli, ginger and five spice and cook, stirring, for 1–2 minutes until fragrant.

Add the tomatoes, soy and 375 ml (13 fl oz/1/½ cups) of water and stir well. Return the lamb shanks to the pan and bring to the boil. Reduce the heat to low, cover and simmer for 1½ hours or until the meat is extremely tender. Stir in the sugar. Check the seasoning and skim off any excess oil.

Serve the shanks with steamed greens, rice and lime wedges.

## MUSSELS WITH WHITE WINE AND LEEK

SERVES 4

1 TABLESPOON OLIVE OIL
1 TABLESPOON BUTTER
1 LEEK, WHITE PART ONLY, THINLY SLICED
2 CELERY STALKS, FINELY DICED
2 GARLIC CLOVES, THINLY SLICED
1.5 KG (3 LB 5 OZ) BLACK MUSSELS, SCRUBBED AND DEBEARDED
185 ML (6 FL OZ/¾ CUP) WHITE WINE
4 THYME SPRIGS
125 ML (4 FL OZ/½ CUP) CREAM

**TO SERVE**
CRUSTY BREAD

Heat the olive oil and butter in a large heavy-based pan over medium heat. Add the leek and celery and cook, stirring occasionally, for 6–7 minutes until the vegetables are soft. Add the garlic and cook, stirring, for 1 minute more.

Add the mussels and stir together gently until well combined. Add the wine and thyme sprigs, cover the pan and simmer for 6–7 minutes. Stir in the cream, cover and simmer for a further 5 minutes or until the mussels are open (discard any that haven't opened in that time). Serve with lots of crusty bread to soak up the sauce.

"You do have to be a bit vigilant with mussels. Before you cook, get rid of any that don't close when you give them a little tap on the kitchen bench."

## CHEAT'S CHIPS

SERVES 2

3 LARGE POTATOES (SUCH AS DESIREE), PEELED AND CUT INTO THICK CHIPS
2 TABLESPOONS OLIVE OIL
SEA SALT
3 TABLESPOONS FINELY GRATED PARMESAN CHEESE
1 TABLESPOON CHOPPED FRESH FLAT-LEAF (ITALIAN) PARSLEY

Preheat the oven to 220°C (425°F/Gas 7). Put the potatoes in a steamer and steam for 7–8 minutes (they will be parcooked and not completely tender).

Toss the chips with the olive oil and spread out in a single layer on a large baking tray. Season with sea salt. Bake for 25–30 minutes, then sprinkle with half the parmesan and the parsley. Return to the oven for a further 5–10 minutes until the chips are crisp and golden. Sprinkle with the remaining parmesan just before serving.

"I love chips and these ones are fantastically easy to make. (Deep-frying scares the life out of me. And what do you do with all that leftover oil?) These are less greasy than the average chip and have the best fluffy centres."

# BEEF IN RED WINE

SERVES 6

1.5 KG (3 LB 5 OZ) CHUCK STEAK, TRIMMED AND CUT INTO SMALL CUBES
5 GARLIC CLOVES, SLICED
1 ONION, CHOPPED
2 CELERY STALKS, CHOPPED
500 ML (17 FL OZ/2 CUPS) RED WINE
400 G (14 OZ) TIN CHOPPED TOMATOES
1 TABLESPOON OLIVE OIL
200 G (7 OZ) FRENCH SHALLOTS, PEELED
150 G (5½ OZ) BACON, RIND REMOVED, CUT INTO BATONS
250 G (9 OZ) BUTTON MUSHROOMS, TRIMMED
3 TEASPOONS CORNFLOUR (CORNSTARCH)
SEA SALT
FRESHLY GROUND BLACK PEPPER
2 TABLESPOONS CHOPPED FRESH FLAT-LEAF (ITALIAN) PARSLEY

TO SERVE
CREAMY MASHED POTATOES

Put the steak, garlic, onion, celery and wine in a large non-metallic bowl, mix together, cover and leave in the fridge to marinate for at least 4 hours, or preferably overnight.

Preheat the oven to 160°C (315°F/Gas 2–3). Tip the beef, the marinade and the tomatoes into a large ovenproof dish, cover and cook in the oven for 2 hours.

Heat the olive oil in a large frying pan over medium-high heat. Add the shallots and cook, stirring occasionally, for 5 minutes or until golden. Add the bacon and mushrooms and cook for a further 3–4 minutes until the bacon is crisp. Mix the cornflour with enough cold water to form a smooth paste. Add the shallots, bacon and mushrooms to the casserole with the cornflour mixture and stir together very well.

Return to the oven for a further 20 minutes, season with salt and pepper and stir through the parsley. If you like the sauce to be thicker, uncover the dish and cook it on the stove top at a high simmer for 5 minutes to reduce the liquid. Serve with some creamy mashed potatoes.

"In cold weather I find myself cooking in quite a different way – a bit more butter, a little more cream and often a good measure of red wine."

# LEG OF LAMB WITH INDIAN FLAVOURS AND TOMATO CHUTNEY

SERVES 4–6

2 KG (4 LB 8 OZ) LEG OF LAMB
125 ML (4 FL OZ/½ CUP) PLAIN YOGHURT
1 GARLIC CLOVE, CRUSHED
3 CM (ABOUT 1 INCH) PIECE OF FRESH GINGER, GRATED
2 TEASPOONS GARAM MASALA
1 TEASPOON CUMIN SEEDS, LIGHTLY TOASTED AND CRUSHED
½ TEASPOON GROUND CINNAMON
SEA SALT
FRESHLY GROUND BLACK PEPPER

**TO SERVE**
TOMATO CHUTNEY, BELOW
TURMERIC-SPICED POTATOES, OPPOSITE
RADISH AND SPINACH SALAD, OPPOSITE

Make slashes all over the leg of lamb and place it in a large roasting tin. Mix the yoghurt, garlic, ginger and spices together well and season with salt and pepper. Rub the marinade all over the lamb, making sure it gets into the slashes. Leave to marinate in a cool place for an hour. Preheat the oven to 190°C (375°F/Gas 5) and roast the lamb for 1½ hours. Remove from the oven and leave to rest for 15–20 minutes before carving. Serve with tomato chutney, turmeric-spiced potatoes and radish and spinach salad.

# TOMATO CHUTNEY

2 TABLESPOONS OLIVE OIL
2 TEASPOONS BLACK MUSTARD SEEDS
2 TEASPOONS TURMERIC
2 TEASPOONS GROUND CUMIN
2 LONG RED CHILLIES, FINELY CHOPPED
2 TABLESPOONS GRATED FRESH GINGER
2 GARLIC CLOVES, CRUSHED
800 G (1 LB 12 OZ) TINNED CHOPPED TOMATOES
100 ML (3½ FL OZ) MALT VINEGAR
85 G (3 OZ/⅓ CUP) BROWN SUGAR
A PINCH OF SEA SALT

Heat the oil in a large saucepan over medium-high heat. Add the mustard seeds, turmeric and cumin and cook, stirring, for 3–4 minutes until fragrant. Add the chilli, ginger and garlic and cook for a further 2–3 minutes. Add the tomatoes, vinegar, sugar and salt and simmer, stirring occasionally, for 1 hour, or until thick.

## TURMERIC-SPICED POTATOES

SERVES 4

800 G (1 LB 12 OZ) YELLOW WAXY POTATOES (SUCH AS NICOLA), PEELED, CUT INTO WEDGES
2 TABLESPOONS OLIVE OIL
30 G (1 OZ) BUTTER, DICED
2 TEASPOONS GROUND TURMERIC
SEA SALT
FRESHLY GROUND BLACK PEPPER
4 SPRING ONIONS (SCALLIONS), FINELY SLICED
2 TABLESPOONS CHOPPED FRESH CORIANDER (CILANTRO)

Preheat the oven to 220°C (425°F/Gas 7). Put the potatoes in a steamer and steam for 10 minutes (they will be parcooked and not completely tender).

Mix the olive oil, butter and turmeric in a large bowl, add the potatoes and toss well so they are thoroughly coated. Season with salt and pepper and arrange the potatoes in a single layer in a large baking tray. Roast for 30–40 minutes, turning once or twice, until golden and crisp. Toss with the spring onion and coriander and serve immediately.

## RADISH AND SPINACH SALAD

SERVES 4

6 RADISHES, TRIMMED
1 TEASPOON SEA SALT
3 TABLESPOONS LIME JUICE
1 TABLESPOON OLIVE OIL
FRESHLY GROUND BLACK PEPPER
100 G (3½ OZ) BABY SPINACH

Slice the radishes very thinly and place in a colander. Sprinkle with sea salt and 2 tablespoons of the lime juice and leave for 5 minutes.

Whisk together the remaining lime juice and the olive oil and season with sea salt and freshly ground black pepper.

Rinse the radishes and pat dry with kitchen paper. Mix the spinach and radishes in a large serving bowl and toss with the dressing.

# STICKY PUDDINGS

## COCONUT RICE PUDDING WITH CARAMELISED PINEAPPLE

SERVES 4

400 ML (14 FL OZ) COCONUT MILK
500 ML (17 FL OZ/2 CUPS) MILK
225 G (8 OZ/1 CUP) ARBORIO RICE
3 TABLESPOONS CASTER (SUPERFINE) SUGAR
1 TEASPOON VANILLA EXTRACT

**TO SERVE**
CARAMELISED PINEAPPLE, BELOW

Preheat the oven to 170°C (325°F/Gas 3) and lightly grease a 1.5 litre (52 fl oz/6 cup) baking dish. Put the coconut milk, milk, rice, sugar and vanilla in the dish and stir together well. Cover with foil and bake for 1¼ hours, then remove the foil and return to the oven for another 30–35 minutes, until nicely browned on top. Leave to rest for 10 minutes before serving with caramelised pineapple.

## CARAMELISED PINEAPPLE

½ TEASPOON GROUND CINNAMON
2 TABLESPOONS BROWN SUGAR
3 THIN SLICES FRESH PINEAPPLE, CUT INTO SMALL TRIANGLES

Mix together the cinnamon and sugar on a large plate. Toss the pineapple triangles in the cinnamon sugar, so they are coated on all sides.

Heat a large non-stick frying pan over medium-high heat and cook the pineapple for 1 minute on each side or until caramelised. Serve with the rice pudding.

"The coconut milk gives this traditional pudding a new twist — great for after spicy food."

## CHOCOLATE ORANGE SELF-SAUCING PUDDING

SERVES 4–6

125 G (4½ OZ/1 CUP) PLAIN (ALL-PURPOSE) FLOUR
A PINCH OF SALT
115 G (4 OZ/½ CUP) CASTER (SUPERFINE) SUGAR
3 TEASPOONS BAKING POWDER
4 TABLESPOONS COCOA POWDER
250 ML (9 FL OZ/1 CUP) MILK
FINELY GRATED ZEST OF 1 ORANGE
85 G (3 OZ) UNSALTED BUTTER, MELTED
2 EGGS, LIGHTLY BEATEN
1 TABLESPOON ORANGE LIQUEUR

**TOPPING**
185 G (6½ OZ/1 CUP) SOFT BROWN SUGAR
2 TABLESPOONS COCOA POWDER
1 TABLESPOON ORANGE LIQUEUR

**TO SERVE**
VANILLA ICE CREAM OR CREAM

Preheat the oven to 180°C (350°F/Gas 4) and grease a 1.5 litre (52 fl oz/6-cup) ovenproof dish. Sift the flour, salt, sugar, baking powder and cocoa powder into a bowl. Add the milk, orange zest, butter, egg and liqueur and beat together well. Pour into the dish.

To make the topping, stir the brown sugar and cocoa powder together and then spread over the pudding batter. Mix the liqueur with 250 ml (9 fl oz/1 cup) of boiling water and pour carefully over the pudding. Bake for 35–40 minutes or until the top of the pudding is firm. Serve with vanilla ice cream or whipped cream.

# STEAMED DATE PUDDINGS WITH CUSTARD

**SERVES 4**

100 G (3½ OZ) UNSALTED BUTTER, SOFTENED
1 TEASPOON VANILLA EXTRACT
100 G (3½ OZ) CASTER (SUPERFINE) SUGAR
2 EGGS, LIGHTLY BEATEN
125 G (4½ OZ/1 CUP) PLAIN (ALL-PURPOSE) FLOUR
2 TEASPOONS BAKING POWDER
½ TEASPOON GROUND CINNAMON
150 ML (5 FL OZ) MILK
125 G (4½ OZ) DATES, FINELY CHOPPED
1 RIPE BANANA, MASHED

**TO SERVE**
CUSTARD, BELOW

Lightly butter four 200 ml (7 fl oz) pudding basins and line the bases with baking paper. Cream the butter, vanilla and sugar together until pale and creamy. Add the eggs a little at a time, beating well after each addition.

Sift the flour, baking powder and cinnamon together and spoon into the batter, alternating with spoonfuls of milk, until both have been added and you have a smooth batter. Stir in the dates and banana. Spoon into the pudding basins.

Cut four pieces of baking paper and fold a thin pleat down the middle of each one. Place a piece over each basin and tie with string. Put the puddings in a steamer over a saucepan of gently simmering water and steam for 40–50 minutes, or until cooked through (check the water level in the saucepan from time to time). Serve with warm custard.

# CUSTARD

250 ML (9 FL OZ/1 CUP) MILK
185 ML (6 FL OZ/¾ CUP) CREAM
1 TEASPOON VANILLA EXTRACT
4 EGG YOLKS
1 EGG
2 TABLESPOONS CASTER (SUPERFINE) SUGAR

Gently heat the milk, cream and vanilla in a small saucepan. Whisk the egg yolks, egg and sugar together in a small bowl, then whisk in the milk mixture until smooth. Tip back into the saucepan and stir over low heat for 10 minutes, or until the custard has thickened. Remove from the heat, cover and keep warm.

I might not have the best memory celebrate in the world but I can always remember when I first made, or first tasted, certain dishes. We all have different ways of slipping bookmarks into our lives and for me it's food that captures the essence of any special moment.

Anyone who's ever organised a wedding will know what a huge feat of planning it can be. When Natalie and I were getting married, the very first thing we decided was that we wanted our guests to enjoy our friend Steven Snow's barbecued seafood. We had not one, but two, meals that day and worked for weeks with Steven until we were happy. After all this tricky planning we felt a touch smug that everything was so perfectly under control. That was until the celebrant asked us about our vows and order of service, and we had to reply quite honestly, 'We've no idea... but the food's all sorted'.

Until then, our biggest and best party had been Millennium Eve. There was a real feeling of armageddon: no one dared go out in case they were attacked by maddened computers. So we invited everyone over and made tapas. I love tapas and I think it's just ideal for a relaxed party of shared plates, which is really my favourite way of entertaining. It was the first time I made semolina-fried school prawns, and they were inspired in a most unexpected way. Years ago, Nat and I were driving to Victoria when our car engine blew up at a little place on the coast called Tathra. Despite the mechanic's gloomy prognosis and the fact that we had to limp into the town centre by taxi, both of us rate the bucket of fresh prawns with mayo that we ate sitting on Tathra's historic wharf as one of the best meals of our lives.

So, in our family, the first thought for any celebration is always, 'What will the food be?' (Which hopefully means our marriage will be a great success.) Our second child, Inès, was a home birth and Natalie had read somewhere about a German woman who painted the house and her rocking chair AND made a cake during labour. So, Nat decided she wanted to make a flourless chocolate cake. Or rather, being a producer, she wanted *me* to make a flourless chocolate cake. I set to it smartly (any recent father reading this will nod sagely), spent a fortune on the best chocolate and had just started melting it, when she rushed into the kitchen, glared at me with that particular fury of a labouring woman and snatched the pan off the heat. Apparently the smell of melting chocolate was not ideal. We finally made the cake a couple of days later and had the midwives over for a slice with a cup of tea. That was a real 'birth' day cake, a beautiful dense adult cake that's too rich for most children, so I've included a few other ideas in here as well. However, in our house the flourless chocolate and hazelnut cake will always be known as THE birthday cake.

# CHRISTMAS

## BUCKWHEAT BLINIS WITH CREME FRAICHE AND SMOKED SALMON

**MAKES ABOUT 25 PIKELET SIZE BLINIS, OR 70 SMALL PARTY BLINIS**

1 TABLESPOON CASTER (SUPERFINE) SUGAR
300 ML (10½ FL OZ) WARM MILK
2 TEASPOONS DRIED YEAST
125 G (4½ OZ/1 CUP) BUCKWHEAT FLOUR
60 G (2¼ OZ/½ CUP) PLAIN (ALL-PURPOSE) FLOUR
½ TEASPOON SALT
2 EGGS, SEPARATED
1 TABLESPOON MELTED BUTTER, PLUS EXTRA TO BRUSH

**TO SERVE**
200 ML (7 FL OZ) CREME FRAICHE
500 G (1 LB 2 OZ) SMOKED SALMON OR GRAVLAX
SNIPPED CHIVES

Stir 1 teaspoon of the sugar into the milk in a small bowl, sprinkle with the yeast and whisk with a fork until the yeast has dissolved. Sift the flours, remaining sugar and salt into a large bowl and make a well in the centre. Whisk the egg yolks into the yeast mixture and pour into the well in the dry ingredients. Whisk until combined. Cover and set aside in a warm place for 45 minutes to 1 hour until doubled in size. Stir the batter a couple of times to knock out most of the air, then cover and leave for another 20–30 minutes.

Stir the melted butter into the batter. Whip the egg whites in a separate clean bowl and then carefully fold into the batter with a metal spoon until just combined.

Heat a large non-stick frying pan over medium heat and brush with melted butter. Drop heaped tablespoons or teaspoons of batter into the pan, depending on what size you want your blinis. Cook for about 1 minute until bubbles appear on the surface of the blinis. Turn the blinis and cook for a further 30 seconds, or until golden. Serve with crème fraiche and gravlax and a few snipped chives.

## PRAWN AND LEMON COCKTAILS WITH CHILLI CORIANDER MAYONNAISE

SERVES 6

24 LARGE COOKED PRAWNS (SHRIMP), PEELED AND DEVEINED, TAILS LEFT INTACT
2 SMALL COS (ROMAINE) LETTUCES, LEAVES SEPARATED
1 AVOCADO, THINLY SLICED
1 LEMON, QUARTERED AND THINLY SLICED

CHILLI CORIANDER MAYONNAISE
170 ML (5½ FL OZ/⅔ CUP) MAYONNAISE
1 LONG RED CHILLI, SEEDED AND FINELY CHOPPED
1 TABLESPOON CHOPPED FRESH CORIANDER (CILANTRO)
1 TABLESPOON LIME JUICE
1 TEASPOON FISH SAUCE
1 TEASPOON FINELY GRATED LIME ZEST

Arrange the prawns, lettuce, avocado and lemon in 6 serving bowls or glasses. Mix together all the ingredients for the chilli coriander mayonnaise and drizzle over the prawn cocktails.

## PRAWN, AVOCADO AND ORANGE SALAD WITH SHALLOT VINAIGRETTE

SERVES 6

1 FRENCH SHALLOT, FINELY CHOPPED
2 TABLESPOONS WHITE WINE VINEGAR
24 LARGE COOKED PRAWNS (SHRIMP), PEELED AND DEVEINED, TAILS LEFT INTACT
1 AVOCADO, DICED
1 BUTTER LETTUCE, ROUGHLY TORN
1 ORANGE, WHITE PITH REMOVED, CUT INTO SEGMENTS
2 TABLESPOONS EXTRA VIRGIN OLIVE OIL

Mix the shallot and vinegar in a small bowl and leave for 5 minutes. Toss together the prawns, avocado, lettuce and orange segments, drizzle with the olive oil and then with the shallot vinegar.

"These are two different versions of the classic prawn cocktail – one spiced-up traditional and the other a fresh California-style salad."

# HOISIN- AND PLUM-GLAZED HAM

SERVES 15 WITH LEFTOVERS

6 KG (13 LB) COOKED LEG HAM
8–10 PIECES STAR ANISE, TO DECORATE
125 ML (4 FL OZ/½ CUP) HOISIN SAUCE
125 ML (4 FL OZ/½ CUP) PLUM SAUCE
3 TABLESPOONS SHAOXING CHINESE RICE WINE
3 TABLESPOONS SOY SAUCE
3 TABLESPOONS BROWN SUGAR
1 TEASPOON CHINESE FIVE SPICE POWDER

Preheat the oven to 180°C (350°F/Gas 4). Use a small sharp knife to cut through the rind around the shank of the ham. Carefully lift the rind from the fat — run your fingers through where the rind and fat join, to help separate them.

Score the white fat in a diamond pattern and press star anise into the centre of every couple of diamonds. Put the ham on a rack over a roasting tin and pour a small amount of water into the tin to prevent the glaze catching on the bottom.

Put the hoisin sauce, plum sauce, rice wine, soy sauce, sugar and five spice in a saucepan over low heat and stir until the sugar has dissolved and everything is combined. Pour the glaze over the ham, making sure that all the white fat is covered. Bake the ham for 30–40 minutes until golden, basting frequently. Remove from the oven and put the ham on a platter.

Transfer the roasting tin to the stovetop over low heat and stir to reduce and thicken the pan juices. Watch very carefully at this stage as the glaze can catch easily. When the liquid is syrupy, pour it over the ham.

The unsliced leftover ham can be stored for a couple of weeks in the fridge, covered with a tea towel. You can also get special cotton ham storage bags from good butchers at Christmas.

## ROASTED POUSSINS WITH RICE AND CHORIZO STUFFING

**SERVES 4**

2 TABLESPOONS OLIVE OIL
1 CHORIZO SAUSAGE, FINELY DICED
1 ONION, FINELY CHOPPED
2 CELERY STALKS, FINELY CHOPPED
2 GARLIC CLOVES, CRUSHED
2 TEASPOONS FINELY GRATED LEMON ZEST
1 TEASPOON PAPRIKA
375 G (13 OZ/2 CUPS) COOKED MEDIUM-GRAIN RICE
2 TABLESPOONS CHOPPED FRESH FLAT-LEAF (ITALIAN) PARSLEY
SEA SALT
FRESHLY GROUND BLACK PEPPER
4 X 500 G (1 LB 2 OZ) POUSSINS (SPATCHCOCKS)

**TO SERVE**
SWEET POTATO WITH CORIANDER AND PRESERVED LEMON, OVERLEAF
GREEN BEAN AND POMEGRANATE SALAD, OVERLEAF

Heat a little of the olive oil in a large frying pan over medium heat and cook the chorizo for
5 minutes or until crisp. Remove the chorizo and add the onion and celery to the pan. Cook, stirring
occasionally, for 5 minutes or until soft. Add the garlic, lemon zest and paprika and cook, stirring,
for 1 minute more. Add the rice, chorizo and parsley, season with sea salt and freshly ground black
pepper and stir together. Remove from the heat and leave to cool.

Preheat the oven to 220°C (425°F/Gas 7). Rinse the cavity of each poussin and pat dry with kitchen
paper. Fill each cavity with the rice stuffing and fasten closed with a toothpick or skewer. Put
the birds on a large baking tray and drizzle with the remaining olive oil. Season well with salt and
pepper and bake for 35–40 minutes, or until the juices run clear when you poke a skewer into
the thickest part of the thigh. Serve with sweet potato with coriander and preserved lemon and green
bean and pomegranate salad.

"Baby chickens are called poussins
in Europe but often known as
spatchcocks in Australia. As
'spatchcock' also means to flatten
the bird, this can cause kitchen
confusion. Don't flatten these ones!"

"Timing can often be a challenge with Christmas dinner. These sweet potatoes work well at room temperature and can sit quite happily on one side while you get everything else ready."

## SWEET POTATO WITH CORIANDER AND PRESERVED LEMON

SERVES 4–6

1 TABLESPOON OLIVE OIL
1 RED ONION, FINELY DICED
2 TEASPOONS GRATED FRESH GINGER
1 TEASPOON GROUND CUMIN
2 TEASPOONS GROUND CORIANDER
1 KG (2 LB 4 OZ) SWEET POTATOES, PEELED AND DICED
SEA SALT
FRESHLY GROUND BLACK PEPPER
1 TABLESPOON CHOPPED FRESH CORIANDER (CILANTRO)
2 PRESERVED LEMON QUARTERS, FLESH AND PITH REMOVED, FINELY DICED

Heat the olive oil in a large deep frying pan over medium heat. Add the onion and cook, stirring occasionally, for 5 minutes. Add the ginger, cumin and coriander and cook, stirring, for another minute. Add the sweet potato and 250 ml (9 fl oz/1 cup) of water to the pan and stir well. Cover, reduce the heat to low and simmer for 12 minutes. Remove the lid and simmer for 5–10 minutes until all the water has evaporated and the sweet potato is tender.

Season with salt and pepper and serve warm or at room temperature, sprinkled with the coriander and preserved lemon.

## GREEN BEAN AND POMEGRANATE SALAD

SERVES 4–6

350 G (12 OZ) SMALL GREEN BEANS, TOPPED BUT NOT TAILED
1 SMALL RED ONION, THINLY SLICED
A HANDFUL OF FRESH FLAT-LEAF (ITALIAN) PARSLEY LEAVES
A HANDFUL OF FRESH MINT LEAVES
SEA SALT
FRESHLY GROUND BLACK PEPPER
POMEGRANATE SEEDS, TO GARNISH

**DRESSING**
2 TABLESPOONS EXTRA VIRGIN OLIVE OIL
1 TABLESPOON POMEGRANATE MOLASSES
1 TABLESPOON LEMON JUICE
A PINCH OF CASTER (SUPERFINE) SUGAR

To make the dressing, whisk together all the ingredients. Blanch the beans for a couple of minutes in a saucepan of lightly salted water until bright green and tender crisp. Rinse under cold running water and drain well. Toss together the beans, onion, parsley and mint, season with salt and pepper, drizzle with the dressing and garnish with pomegranate seeds.

# VERY EASY PLUM PUDDINGS WITH BRANDY SAUCE

**SERVES 10**

300 G (10½ OZ) RAISINS
100 G (3½ OZ) SULTANAS
100 G (3½ OZ) CURRANTS
100 G (3½ OZ) GLACE FRUIT (FIGS, APRICOTS OR CHERRIES)
150 G (5½ OZ) UNSALTED BUTTER
1 TEASPOON BICARBONATE OF SODA
175 G (6 OZ) BROWN SUGAR
1 TABLESPOON MARMALADE
3 TABLESPOONS BRANDY
300 G (10½ OZ) PLAIN (ALL-PURPOSE) FLOUR
2 TEASPOONS BAKING POWDER
1 TEASPOON MIXED SPICE
1 TABLESPOON COCOA POWDER
2 EGGS, LIGHTLY BEATEN

**TO SERVE**
BRANDY SAUCE, BELOW

Preheat the oven to 180°C (350°F/Gas 4). Grease ten 200 ml (7 fl oz) muffin tins or dariole moulds. Heat the dried and glacé fruit, butter, bicarbonate of soda, sugar, marmalade, 1 tablespoon of the brandy and 250 ml (9 fl oz/1 cup) of water in a saucepan. Bring to the boil, stirring constantly, then allow to cool.

Sift together the flour, baking powder, mixed spice and cocoa. Add the eggs to the cooled fruit mixture, then add the flour mix and stir together. Spoon into the tins or moulds and bake for 25–30 minutes, or until a skewer comes out clean when you poke it into the centre. Remove from the oven and pour the rest of the brandy over the puddings while they're still warm. Serve with brandy sauce.

# BRANDY SAUCE

600 ML (21 FL OZ) MILK
1 VANILLA BEAN, SPLIT, SEEDS SCRAPED
60 G (2¼ OZ) CASTER (SUPERFINE) SUGAR
2 TABLESPOONS CORNFLOUR (CORNSTARCH), MIXED WITH 4 TABLESPOONS COLD MILK
50 G (1¾ OZ) BUTTER
1 TABLESPOON BRANDY

Put the milk, vanilla bean and seeds, and sugar in a small pan and bring to a gentle boil. Stir in the cornflour mixture and keep stirring until thickened. Stir in the butter and brandy.

## FRESH MANGO AND MACADAMIA TRIFLES WITH LIME SYRUP

SERVES 12

330 G (11 OZ/1½ CUPS) CASTER (SUPERFINE) SUGAR
125 ML (4 FL OZ/½ CUP) LIME JUICE
300 ML (10½ FL OZ) THICK GREEK YOGHURT
300 ML (10½ FL OZ) LIGHTLY WHIPPED CREAM
3 TABLESPOONS ICING (CONFECTIONER'S) SUGAR, SIFTED
1½ TEASPOONS VANILLA EXTRACT
MACADAMIA CAKE, BELOW, CUT INTO CUBES
4 LARGE MANGOES, SLICED
125 G (4½ OZ/¾ CUP) UNSALTED MACADAMIA NUTS, CHOPPED

To make the lime syrup, put the sugar, lime juice and 185 ml (6 fl oz/¾ cup) of water in a saucepan over medium heat and cook, stirring, until the sugar has dissolved. Increase the heat to high, bring to the boil, then reduce the heat and simmer for 10 minutes or until slightly reduced. Set aside to cool.

Whisk together the yoghurt, cream, icing sugar and vanilla until well combined. Place half the sponge cubes into 12 individual serving dishes or one large glass dish. Drizzle with half the lime syrup and top with half the mango slices, then half the whipped vanilla cream. Repeat the layers one more time to use up all the ingredients, and sprinkle the tops with macadamia nuts.


## MACADAMIA CAKE

160 G (5¾ OZ/1 CUP) UNSALTED MACADAMIA NUTS
6 EGGS, SEPARATED
220 G (7 OZ/1 CUP) CASTER (SUPERFINE) SUGAR
185 ML (6½ FL OZ/¾ CUP) PLAIN YOGHURT
125 ML (4 FL OZ/½ CUP) GRAPESEED OIL (OR OTHER LIGHT-FLAVOURED OIL)
150 G (5½ OZ) PLAIN (ALL-PURPOSE) FLOUR, SIFTED
1 TEASPOON BAKING POWDER

Preheat the oven to 180°C (350°F/Gas 4). Lightly grease and line the base of a 22 x 32 cm (about 9 x 12 inch) baking tray with baking paper.

Finely grind the macadamia nuts in a food processor. Place the egg yolks in a bowl with half the sugar and beat with electric beaters until pale and very thick. Mix in the yoghurt and oil, then fold in the ground macadamias, flour, baking powder and a pinch of salt.

In a separate bowl, beat the egg whites with electric beaters until soft peaks form, then add the remaining caster sugar and beat until stiff peaks form and the mixture is glossy. Gently fold half the egg white into the macadamia mixture with a metal spoon, then fold in the other half.

Pour into the baking tray and bake for 25 minutes, or until light golden. Leave to cool in the tray for 10 minutes before turning out onto a wire rack to cool completely.

## ZUPPA INGLESE

SERVES 6

125 ML (4 FL OZ/½ CUP) ESPRESSO COFFEE
125 ML (4 FL OZ/½ CUP) COFFEE LIQUEUR
2 TABLESPOONS COGNAC, OR BRANDY
VANILLA CUSTARD CREAM, BELOW
1 X 16 CM (6 INCH) ROUND SPONGE CAKE, CUT INTO 1 CM (½ INCH) SLICES
CHOCOLATE CUSTARD CREAM, BELOW
FINELY GRATED DARK CHOCOLATE OR UNSWEETENED COCOA POWDER, TO DUST

Stir together the espresso, liqueur and Cognac. You can make zuppa inglese in one large glass
dish or 6 individual bowls or glasses (glasses are always best because they allow you to see the layers).

Start with a little vanilla custard at the bottom of each dish and top with a layer of cake slices.
Moisten the cake generously by spooning over the espresso mixture. Follow this with a layer
of chocolate custard.  Repeat the cake soaked with espresso mixture, and top with vanilla custard.
Repeat the layers until all the cake and custard has been used, finishing with a layer of custard.

Chill for at least 4 hours, or overnight. Dust with dark chocolate or cocoa powder to serve.

## VANILLA AND CHOCOLATE CUSTARD CREAM

6 EGG YOLKS
60 G (2¼ OZ/½ CUP) ICING (CONFECTIONER'S) SUGAR
2 TABLESPOONS PLAIN (ALL-PURPOSE) FLOUR
750 ML (26 FL OZ/3 CUPS) MILK
½ TEASPOON VANILLA EXTRACT
100 G (3½ OZ) DARK CHOCOLATE, FINELY CHOPPED

Put the egg yolks and sugar in a stainless steel bowl and beat until pale yellow and creamy. Add the
flour and beat until well combined. Put the milk in a saucepan over medium-high heat and bring
almost to the boil. Remove from the heat and gradually pour into the egg mixture, beating all the
time.  Place the bowl over a simmering pan of water and cook for 8–10 minutes, stirring constantly
until the custard has thickened.

Remove from the heat and divide the custard into two separate bowls. Add the vanilla extract to one
bowl to make vanilla custard cream. Add the chocolate to the other bowl and stir until it has melted.

## WHITE CHOCOLATE, CHERRY AND ALMOND NOUGAT

**MAKES 45 PIECES**

EDIBLE RICE PAPER
460 G (1 LB/2 CUPS) CASTER (SUPERFINE) SUGAR
250 ML (9 FL OZ/1 CUP) GLUCOSE SYRUP
125 ML (4 FL OZ/½ CUP) HONEY
1 TEASPOON VANILLA EXTRACT
2 EGG WHITES
125 G (4½ OZ) BLANCHED ALMONDS, LIGHTLY TOASTED
150 G (5½ OZ) WHITE CHOCOLATE, CHOPPED
100 G (3½ OZ) DRIED CHERRIES

Lightly grease a 20 x 30 cm (8 x 12 inch) baking tray and line with sheets of edible rice paper. Put the sugar, glucose, honey and vanilla in a large heavy-based saucepan and cook, stirring constantly, over low heat until the sugar has dissolved. Bring to the boil, then boil without stirring, brushing down the side of the saucepan with a wet pastry brush to remove any sugar crystals which may form. Cook until the mixture reaches 142°C (275°F) on a sugar thermometer (soft crack stage), or test the syrup by dropping a small teaspoonful into a bowl of iced water — you should be able to remove the ball of syrup and stretch it with your fingers into pliable strands.

Meanwhile, beat the egg whites in a large clean bowl until firm peaks form. While beating, very slowly pour the hot syrup in a thin stream into the egg white. Continue to beat until the mixture is thick and holds its shape — depending on your beaters, this could take between 2 and 8 minutes. Once the mixture can hold its shape, stop beating. You don't want it to thicken too much and become like toffee. Gently warm the nuts in a dry pan. Stir into the mixture with the chocolate and cherries.

Pour the mixture into the tin and place a layer of rice paper over the top. Leave to set overnight and then cut into squares or bars with a hot, wet knife.

"You'll need someone with a strong arm to stir the fruit and nuts through this nougat. Dried cranberries will also work well, if you can't find cherries."

# WEDDING LUNCH

## MIXED SEAFOOD WITH PAPRIKA AND LEMON DRESSING

**SERVES 6**

1 KG (2 LB 4 OZ) BABY SQUID, CLEANED
1 KG (2 LB 4 OZ) LARGE RAW PRAWNS (SHRIMP), PEELED AND DEVEINED, TAILS LEFT INTACT
6 X 150 G (5½ OZ) FIRM WHITE FISH FILLETS
2 TABLESPOONS OLIVE OIL

**PAPRIKA AND LEMON DRESSING**
JUICE AND FINELY GRATED ZEST OF 1 LEMON
3 GARLIC CLOVES, VERY THINLY SLICED
2 TEASPOONS PAPRIKA
2 TABLESPOONS CHOPPED FRESH FLAT-LEAF (ITALIAN) PARSLEY LEAVES
3 TABLESPOONS EXTRA VIRGIN OLIVE OIL

**TO SERVE**
LEMON WEDGES
RED PEPPER, CORIANDER AND WALNUT RELISH, OVERLEAF
PILAF WITH WHITE WINE AND BAY, OVERLEAF

Cut the squid into 5 cm (2 inch) squares and score the inside. Put the squid, prawns and fish in a large dish, drizzle with 2 tablespoons of the olive oil and mix gently until the seafood is well coated.

Preheat a barbecue chargrill plate to hot and then place the seafood on the plate. Cook the prawns and squid for 1–2 minutes on each side, or until just cooked (be careful not to overcook the squid or it will become tough). Cook the fish for 2 minutes on each side, or until just cooked through.

To make the dressing, mix together the lemon juice, zest, garlic, paprika, parsley and olive oil. Arrange the seafood on a large serving platter, pour the dressing over the top and serve with lemon wedges, red pepper, coriander and walnut relish and the pilaf.

## RED PEPPER, CORIANDER AND WALNUT RELISH

SERVES 6

1 TEASPOON CUMIN SEEDS
1 TEASPOON CORIANDER SEEDS
3 RED CAPSICUMS (PEPPERS), ROASTED, SEEDED AND PEELED
2 LONG RED CHILLIES, SEEDED AND CHOPPED
2 GARLIC CLOVES, CRUSHED
55 G (2 OZ/½ CUP) WALNUTS, LIGHTLY TOASTED
80 ML (2¾ FL OZ/⅓ CUP) EXTRA VIRGIN OLIVE OIL
2 TABLESPOONS CHOPPED FRESH CORIANDER (CILANTRO)
SEA SALT
FRESHLY GROUND BLACK PEPPER

Put the cumin and coriander seeds in a small frying pan over medium heat and roast for 1–2 minutes until fragrant. Remove and grind with a mortar and pestle or spice grinder.

Put the roasted capsicum, chilli, garlic, walnuts and roasted spices in a food processor and pulse until finely chopped. Add the olive oil and coriander and pulse again to mix, adding a little more oil if necessary. The texture should be quite chunky. Season to taste with salt and black pepper.

## PILAF WITH WHITE WINE AND BAY

**SERVES 6**

750 ML (26 FL OZ/3 CUPS) CHICKEN STOCK
1 TABLESPOON OLIVE OIL
20 G (¾ OZ) BUTTER
1 ONION, FINELY CHOPPED
½ TEASPOON SEA SALT
2 GARLIC CLOVES, CRUSHED
400 G (14 OZ) BASMATI RICE, RINSED
125 ML (4 FL OZ/½ CUP) WHITE WINE
2 BAY LEAVES

Put the chicken stock in a saucepan and bring to simmering point. Heat the olive oil and butter in a large heavy-based saucepan over medium heat. Add the onion and salt and cook, stirring occasionally, for 5 minutes. Add the garlic and cook, stirring, for 1 minute more.

Add the rice and stir to coat the grains of rice in the butter. Add the wine and allow to bubble until almost all the wine has evaporated. Add the bay leaves and hot stock and bring to simmering point.

Cover with a tight-fitting lid, reduce the heat to very low and cook for 10 minutes. Turn off the heat, place a tea towel under the lid and set aside for 10 minutes. Fluff with a fork before serving.

"As simple and plain as this looks, a good chicken stock raises it to the sublime. It's a great example of what you can do with a few top-quality ingredients."

NATALIE & BILL

## CHOCOLATE CARAMEL SLICE

**MAKES ABOUT 20 SQUARES**

125 G (4½ OZ/1 CUP) PLAIN (ALL-PURPOSE) FLOUR
1 TEASPOON BAKING POWDER
90 G (3 OZ/1 CUP) DESICCATED COCONUT
115 G (4 OZ/½ CUP) CASTER (SUPERFINE) SUGAR
125 G (4½ OZ) UNSALTED BUTTER, MELTED

**FILLING**
100 G (3½ OZ) UNSALTED BUTTER
100 G (3½ OZ) BROWN SUGAR
400 ML (14 FL OZ) TIN CONDENSED MILK
2 TABLESPOONS GOLDEN SYRUP
1 TEASPOON VANILLA EXTRACT

**TOPPING**
150 G (5½ OZ) GOOD DARK CHOCOLATE
1 TEASPOON FLAKED SEA SALT (SUCH AS MALDON SEA SALT)

Preheat the oven to 180°C (350°F/Gas 4) and lightly grease and line an 18 x 28 cm (7 x 11 inch) baking tin.

Sift the flour and baking powder into a large bowl, add the coconut, sugar and butter and stir together well. Press firmly into the base of the tin and bake for 12 minutes, or until light golden.

To make the filling, put the butter, brown sugar, condensed milk, golden syrup and vanilla in a saucepan over low heat. Cook, stirring, until the sugar has dissolved. Bring to the boil, then reduce the heat to low and cook, stirring, for 5 minutes, or until light golden. Pour evenly over the cooked base, then return to the oven and bake for 10 minutes. Set aside to cool completely.

Once the caramel is cool, put the chocolate in a heatproof bowl over a saucepan of gently simmering water, stirring occasionally until the chocolate has melted (or melt the chocolate very carefully in a microwave oven). Spread the chocolate evenly over the caramel. Once the chocolate has set, sprinkle with the sea salt and cut into squares.

"The sea salt sprinkled over the chocolate makes this a caramel slice for grown-ups."

# TAPAS PARTY

## TOMATO AND CHORIZO SALAD

**SERVES 4 AS A SHARED PLATE**

1½ TABLESPOONS EXTRA VIRGIN OLIVE OIL
2 CHORIZO SAUSAGES, SLICED
250 G (9 OZ) CHERRY OR GRAPE TOMATOES, HALVED
1 SMALL RED ONION, CUT INTO THIN RINGS
1 TABLESPOON SHERRY VINEGAR OR RED WINE VINEGAR
1 TABLESPOON CHOPPED FRESH FLAT-LEAF (ITALIAN) PARSLEY LEAVES
A SQUEEZE OF LEMON JUICE

**TO SERVE**
CRUSTY BREAD

Heat a touch of the olive oil in a large frying pan over medium heat and cook the chorizo for
5 minutes or until crisp. Tip the chorizo into a serving bowl with the cherry tomatoes and red onion.
Whisk together the remaining olive oil and the sherry vinegar to make a dressing. Pour over the
chorizo and tomatoes and toss well. Sprinkle with the parsley and squeeze over a little lemon juice.
Serve with crusty bread to mop up the juices.

## CHARGRILLED BABY OCTOPUS WITH SHERRY VINEGAR DRESSING

**SERVES 6–8 AS A SHARED PLATE**

24 BABY OCTOPUS, CLEANED AND HALVED
2 GARLIC CLOVES, THINLY SLICED
1 LONG RED CHILLI, SEEDED AND CUT INTO LONG STRIPS
JUICE AND ZEST OF 1 LEMON
80 ML (2¾ FL OZ/⅓ CUP) EXTRA VIRGIN OLIVE OIL, PLUS 2 TABLESPOONS EXTRA
2 TABLESPOONS SHERRY VINEGAR

**TO SERVE**
LEMON WEDGES

Put the octopus in a bowl with the garlic, chilli, lemon juice and zest and olive oil. Stir together,
cover and refrigerate for up to 2 hours (don't leave for any longer or the octopus will start to 'cook'
in the marinade).

Whisk together the extra olive oil and the sherry vinegar to make a dressing. Heat a chargrill pan
to high. Drain the octopus from the marinade and chargrill for 2 minutes on each side or until lightly
charred. Pile the octopus onto a serving plate and drizzle with the sherry vinegar dressing. Serve
with lemon wedges.

## PATATAS BRAVAS

**SERVES 4–6 AS A SHARED PLATE**

1.5 KG (3 LB 5 OZ) WAXY POTATOES, PEELED AND DICED
2 TABLESPOONS OLIVE OIL
SEA SALT

**TO SERVE**
BRAVAS SAUCE, BELOW

Bring a large saucepan of water to the boil and add the potato. Bring back to the boil and cook for 5 minutes or until just tender. Rinse under cold running water, drain well and set aside to dry.

Heat the olive oil in a large non-stick frying pan over medium heat. Add the potatoes and fry, stirring occasionally, for 12 minutes, or until the potatoes are golden and crispy. Sprinkle with sea salt and serve with bravas sauce.

## BRAVAS SAUCE

2 TABLESPOONS OLIVE OIL
1 ONION, FINELY CHOPPED
2 GARLIC CLOVES, THINLY SLICED
1 TEASPOON SMOKED SPANISH PAPRIKA
1 TEASPOON PAPRIKA
A PINCH OF CAYENNE PEPPER
1 TEASPOON SUGAR
400 G (14 OZ) TIN CHOPPED TOMATOES

Heat the olive oil in a large saucepan over medium-low heat. Add the onion and cook, stirring occasionally, for 5 minutes or until soft. Add the garlic and cook, stirring, for 2–3 minutes. Add the spices and cook for 1 minute, stirring all the time. Add the sugar and tomatoes, bring to a low simmer and cook for 10–15 minutes until the sauce has thickened.

## SEMOLINA-FRIED SCHOOL PRAWNS WITH SIMPLE AIOLI

**SERVES 6–8 AS A SHARED PLATE**

**250 G (9 OZ/2 CUPS) FINE SEMOLINA**
**2 TEASPOONS PAPRIKA**
**600 G (1 LB 5 OZ) SCHOOL PRAWNS (BABY SHRIMP)**
**GRAPESEED OIL (OR OTHER LIGHT-FLAVOURED OIL), TO DEEP-FRY**

**TO SERVE**
**SEA SALT AND LEMON WEDGES**
**AIOLI, BELOW**

Mix together the semolina and paprika in a large bowl. Add the prawns and toss to coat them well. Tip the prawns into a colander, shaking off the excess semolina.

Heat the oil in deep saucepan or wok to 180°C (350°F) — if you don't have a thermometer, lower a small cube of bread into the oil. It should brown in about 15 seconds. Carefully lower the prawns in batches into the hot oil and cook for 1 minute, or until the prawns change colour and begin to float to the top of the oil. Use a slotted spoon to lift out the prawns and then drain them on kitchen paper. Serve immediately with sea salt, lemon wedges and aioli.

## SIMPLE AIOLI

**MAKES 125 ML (4 FL OZ/½ CUP)**

**125 ML (4 FL OZ/½ CUP) GOOD WHOLE-EGG MAYONNAISE**
**2 GARLIC CLOVES, CRUSHED**

Mix together the mayonnaise and garlic.

"School prawns are the gorgeously sweet tiny prawns whose shells are so crispy and thin they don't even need peeling before you eat them."

"As well as great party food, this tomato bread is actually one of our favourite meals. It's the sort of thing we have for a too-exhausted-to-cook dinner with a glass of wine when the kids have gone to bed."

## TOMATO-RUBBED BREAD

**SERVES 6 AS A SHARED PLATE**

**12 SLICES WOOD-FIRED BREAD**
**EXTRA VIRGIN OLIVE OIL**
**GARLIC CLOVES, HALVED**
**RIPE TOMATOES, HALVED**

**TO SERVE**
**JAMON**
**MANCHEGO**
**MARINATED OLIVES**

Preheat the oven to 200°C (400°F/Gas 6). Brush each slice of bread with olive oil and place on a large baking tray. Bake for 5–10 minutes, turning once, until the bread is golden.

Rub one side of the bread with the cut side of the garlic and then rub with the cut side of the tomato, letting the tomato juice soak into the bread. Serve with jamon, manchego and marinated olives.

## WHITE ANCHOVY, FENNEL AND CELERY SALAD

**SERVES 4–6 AS A SHARED PLATE**

**2 SMALL COS (ROMAINE) LETTUCES, LEAVES SEPARATED**
**1 SMALL FENNEL BULB, OUTER LAYER REMOVED, HALVED AND VERY THINLY SLICED**
**3 CELERY STALKS, THINLY SLICED ON THE DIAGONAL**
**A HANDFUL OF LEAVES FROM THE CELERY HEART**
**2 TABLESPOONS EXTRA VIRGIN OLIVE OIL**
**1 TABLESPOON LEMON JUICE**
**12 WHITE ANCHOVIES**
**FRESHLY GROUND BLACK PEPPER**

Toss together the lettuce, fennel, celery and celery leaves in a large bowl. Whisk together the olive oil and lemon juice. Add the dressing to the salad and gently toss to coat all the leaves. Pile the salad onto a serving platter and garnish with the white anchovies. Season with black pepper.

# GARLIC MUSHROOMS

**SERVES 4 AS A SHARED PLATE**

3 TABLESPOONS OLIVE OIL
350 G (12 OZ) SMALL BUTTON MUSHROOMS
3 GARLIC CLOVES, THINLY SLICED
1 LONG RED CHILLI, SEEDED AND FINELY CHOPPED
SEA SALT
FRESHLY GROUND BLACK PEPPER
1 TABLESPOON CHOPPED FRESH FLAT-LEAF (ITALIAN) PARSLEY

**TO SERVE**
**CRUSTY BREAD**

Heat the oil in a large frying pan over high heat. Add the mushrooms and cook, stirring occasionally, for 2–3 minutes until golden. Remove from the pan.

Put the pan back over medium heat, add the garlic and chilli and cook, stirring, for 1 minute, or until the garlic is light golden. Return the mushrooms to the pan and cook for another 1–2 minutes, stirring to coat well with the garlic.

Remove from the heat and season with sea salt and pepper. Sprinkle with parsley and serve immediately with crusty bread.

# HAPPY BIRTHDAY

## PASSIONFRUIT SPONGE

**SERVES 10–12**

175 G (6 OZ) PLAIN (ALL-PURPOSE) FLOUR
2½ TEASPOONS BAKING POWDER
2 TABLESPOONS CORNFLOUR (CORNSTARCH)
4 EGGS, AT ROOM TEMPERATURE
200 G (7 OZ) CASTER (SUPERFINE) SUGAR
30 G (1 OZ) UNSALTED BUTTER, MELTED
200 ML (7 FL OZ) WHIPPED CREAM

**PASSIONFRUIT ICING**
125 G (4½ OZ/1 CUP) ICING (CONFECTIONER'S) SUGAR
30 G (1 OZ) UNSALTED BUTTER, MELTED
1½ TABLESPOONS PASSIONFRUIT PULP

Preheat the oven to 180°C (350°F/Gas 4) and grease and line two 20 cm (8 inch) sandwich tins. Mix the flour, baking powder and cornflour and sift together twice. Beat the eggs and sugar for about 7–8 minutes, until pale and thick. Gently fold the flour into the beaten eggs.

Mix the butter with 80 ml (2½ fl oz/⅓ cup) of boiling water and then add to the mixture, stirring gently. Divide between the tins and bake for 20 minutes, or until golden and coming away from the the tins. Cool for 10 minutes in the tins before turning out onto a wire rack to cool completely.

To make the passionfruit icing, beat together all the ingredients. Put one of the cakes on a serving plate and spread with whipped cream. Top with the other cake and spread that with the passionfruit icing.

# FLOURLESS CHOCOLATE AND HAZELNUT CAKE

**SERVES 8**

200 G (7 OZ) DARK CHOCOLATE, CHOPPED
125 G (4½ OZ) UNSALTED BUTTER
225 G (8 OZ/1 FIRMLY PACKED CUP) BROWN SUGAR
100 G (3½ OZ) HAZELNUT MEAL (GROUND HAZELNUTS)
5 EGGS, SEPARATED
1 TABLESPOON SIFTED COCOA POWDER

**CINNAMON CREAM**
250 ML (9 FL OZ/1 CUP) THICK (DOUBLE) CREAM
1 TABLESPOON ICING (CONFECTIONER'S) SUGAR, SIFTED
1 TEASPOON GROUND CINNAMON

Preheat the oven to 180°C (350°F/Gas 4) and grease and line the base and sides of a 20 cm (8 inch) springform tin.

Put the chocolate and butter in a heatproof bowl over a saucepan of simmering water (making sure the base of the bowl is not touching the water). Stir occasionally until the chocolate and butter have melted. Remove from the heat and set aside to cool slightly.

Add the sugar and hazelnut meal to the melted chocolate and stir until there are no lumps. Add the egg yolks one at a time, stirring well after each addition. In a clean bowl, whisk the egg whites until firm peaks form. Gently fold the egg whites into the chocolate mixture.

Spoon the mixture into the tin and bake for 45–50 minutes until firm. Leave to cool completely in the tin before removing the side of the tin. Dust the top with cocoa powder.

To make the cinnamon cream, whip the cream, then mix in the icing sugar and cinnamon until well combined. Serve with the cake.

"The golden rule for cooking with chocolate is to use the same quality you'd like to eat straight from the packet."

## NEVER-FAIL BIRTHDAY CHOCOLATE CAKE WITH CHOCOLATE ICING

**SERVES 16**

250 G (9 OZ) UNSALTED BUTTER, SOFTENED
440 G (15½ OZ/2 CUPS) SUGAR
4 EGGS
250 ML (9 FL OZ/1 CUP) MILK
310 G (11 OZ/2½ CUPS) PLAIN (ALL-PURPOSE) FLOUR
5 TEASPOONS BAKING POWDER
4 TABLESPOONS COCOA POWDER
1 TEASPOON VANILLA EXTRACT

**TO DECORATE**
CHOCOLATE ICING, BELOW

Preheat the oven to 180°C (350°F/Gas 4). Grease and line a 20 x 30 cm (8 x 12 inch) cake tin.

Beat the butter, sugar, eggs, milk, flour, baking powder, cocoa powder and vanilla with electric beaters for 8–10 minutes until the mixture is pale and well combined. Pour into the tin and bake for 40–45 minutes, or until a skewer poked into the middle comes out clean. Leave to cool in the tin for 10 minutes, before transferring to a wire rack. Ice with chocolate icing when completely cool.

## CHOCOLATE ICING

300 G (10½ OZ) ICING (CONFECTIONER'S) SUGAR
4 TABLESPOONS COCOA
2 TABLESPOONS SOFTENED UNSALTED BUTTER

Sift together the icing sugar and cocoa. Add the butter and 3–4 tablespoons of warm water and beat until smooth and fluffy, adding more water if necessary.

## LIME AND MANGO CAKE

SERVES 8–10

300 G (10½ OZ) PLAIN (ALL-PURPOSE) FLOUR
2½ TEASPOONS BAKING POWDER
180 G (6 OZ) UNSALTED BUTTER, SOFTENED AND ROUGHLY DICED
250 G (9 OZ) CASTER (SUPERFINE) SUGAR
1½ TEASPOONS FINELY GRATED LIME ZEST
4 EGGS
200 ML (7 FL OZ) PLAIN YOGHURT
1 LARGE MANGO, DICED

TO DECORATE
LIME ICING, BELOW
SHREDDED LIME ZEST

Preheat the oven to 170°C (325°F/Gas 3) and grease a 26 cm (10½ inch) ring tin.

Sift the flour and baking powder together. Beat together the butter, sugar and lime zest until pale and creamy. Add the eggs one at a time, beating well after each addition. Fold in the flour, alternating with the yoghurt, in two batches.

Gently fold the mango through the batter and pour into the tin, smoothing the surface. Bake for 45 minutes, or until a skewer poked into the middle comes out clean. Leave to cool in the tin for 5 minutes before turning out onto a wire rack to cool completely. Drizzle generously with lime icing and decorate with shredded lime zest.

## LIME ICING

185 G (6½ OZ/1½ CUPS) ICING (CONFECTIONER'S) SUGAR
2 TABLESPOONS LIME JUICE
1 TABLESPOON UNSALTED BUTTER, MELTED AND COOLED

Beat together all the ingredients for 30 seconds, or until smooth. The icing should be of a pouring consistency: if it's too thick, add a touch more lime juice.

"If you don't have a ring tin, this will also work in a 22 cm (9 inch) round springform tin."

# ICINGS AND FROSTINGS

## CREAM CHEESE FROSTING

**ICES 2 SMALL OR 1 LARGE CAKE**

500 G (1 LB 2 OZ) CREAM CHEESE, SOFTENED AND CUT INTO SMALL PIECES
3 TABLESPOONS UNSALTED BUTTER, SOFTENED AND CUT INTO SMALL PIECES
2 TEASPOONS VANILLA EXTRACT
250 G (9 OZ/2 CUPS) ICING (CONFECTIONER'S) SUGAR, SIFTED

Beat together the cream cheese, butter and vanilla until smooth. Gradually add the icing sugar and beat until well combined.

## WHIPPED CHOCOLATE BUTTERCREAM

**ICES 2 SMALL OR 1 LARGE CAKE**

200 G (7 OZ) UNSALTED BUTTER, SOFTENED
200 G (7 OZ) MILK CHOCOLATE, MELTED AND COOLED
1 TEASPOON VANILLA EXTRACT
250 G (9 OZ/2 CUPS) ICING (CONFECTIONER'S) SUGAR, SIFTED
2 TABLESPOONS COCOA POWDER, SIFTED

Beat the butter with electric beaters for 3–4 minutes until smooth and creamy. Add the melted chocolate and beat until smooth. Add the vanilla, then gradually add the icing sugar and cocoa and beat until creamy and well combined.

## BUTTERSCOTCH FROSTING

**ICES 2 SMALL OR 1 LARGE CAKE**

125 G (4½ OZ) UNSALTED BUTTER
220 G (7¾ OZ/1 CUP) BROWN SUGAR
80 ML (2½ FL OZ/⅓ CUP) MILK
310 G (11 OZ/2½ CUPS) ICING (CONFECTIONER'S) SUGAR, SIFTED

Put the butter and sugar in a pan over low heat and stir until the sugar has dissolved. Bring to the boil, then simmer for 2–3 minutes. Stir in the milk and set aside to cool. Once cool, add the icing sugar and beat until thick and smooth.

# INDEX

# FOR NATALIE, EDIE, INES AND BUNNY

Published by Murdoch Books Pty Limited.

Murdoch Books Pty Limited Australia
Pier 8/9, 23 Hickson Road, Millers Point NSW 2000
Phone: +61 (0)2 8220 2000  Fax: +61 (0)2 8220 2558
murdochbooks.com.au

Murdoch Books UK Limited
Erico House, 6th Floor, 93–99 Upper Richmond Road
Putney, London SW15 2TG
Phone: +44 (0)20 8785 5995  Fax: +44 (0)20 8785 5985
murdochbooks.com.uk

Chief Executive: Juliet Rogers
Publisher: Kay Scarlett

Photographer: Petrina Tinslay
Stylist: Rebecca Cohen
Stylist's Assistant: Kathryn Burton
Food Preparation and Styling: Chrissy Freer
Food Assistant: Christopher Tate

Editor: Jane Price
Designer: Lauren Camilleri
Design Concept and Art Direction: Richard Ferretti and Erika Oliveira
Production: Kita George

The publisher thanks the following for their generosity in supplying furniture, props, appliances and kitchenware: Accoutrement; Afghan Interiors; All Hand Made Gallery; Bison Australia; Wooden Stencil by Bride&Wolfe; Chee Soon Fitzgerald; Clay and Flax; Cloth; Mark Conway; Country Road; Riess supplied by Crowley & Grouch; Covo Authentics D-Bros Royal VKB Gaia & Gino supplied by dedece+; Dinosaur Designs; Granite & Marble Works; Herbie's Spices; Ici et la; Boda Nova Hoganas Rosendahl Stelton supplied by Jarass; Simon Johnson Purveyor of Quality Foods; Kas Australia; Ken Neale 20th Century Modern; Kif Kaf; Leveson's Hired Interiors; KitchenAid, Zero, Rocket supplied by Peter McInnes; Major & Tom; Mao & More; Miele: Mokum; Mud Australia; Alex Liddy Baccarat Arcosteel supplied by PlayCorp Group of Companies; Porch; Publisher Textiles; Ruby Star Traders; Scanpan Chasseur Bodum WMF Mundial Avanti Brabantia supplied by Sheldon and Hammond; Universal Enterprises; Coza French Bull supplied by Until; Villeroy & Boch; Jasper Conran, Vera Wang supplied by Waterford Wedgwood; Weber Barbeques; Mario Batali supplied by Zoratto Enterprises.

Also, many thanks to Pacific Palms Holidays (02 6554 0500 / www.pacificpalmsholidays.com.au) for photography at Sugarloaf, Seal Rocks (thanks to the Ilic family); Lumina, Smiths Lake; and SaltRock, Boomerang Beach.

Mixed seafood with paprika and lemon dressing, red pepper, coriander and walnut relish and pilaf with white wine and bay (pages 222–5) first appeared in Bon Appetit, May 2007.

National Library of Australia Cataloguing-in-Publication Data
Granger, Bill, 1969- .   Holiday. Includes index. ISBN 978 1 92125 976 0 (hbk).  1. Cookery. I. Title. 641.5

Printed by 1010 Printing International Limited in 2007. PRINTED IN CHINA. First published 2007.

COOKING NOTES: You may find cooking times vary depending on the oven you are using. For fan-forced ovens, as a general rule, set the oven temperature to 20°C (35°F) lower than indicated in the recipe.
We have used 20 ml (4 teaspoon) tablespoon measures. If you are using a 15 ml (3 teaspoon) tablespoon, for most recipes the difference will not be noticeable. However, for recipes using baking powder, gelatine, bicarbonate of soda (baking soda) or small amounts of cornflour (cornstarch), add an extra teaspoon for each tablespoon specified.
We have used 59 g (2 oz) eggs.